Entrepreneurial
DNA

The Breakthrough Discovery that Aligns Your Business to Your Unique Strengths

JOE ABRAHAM

New York   Chicago   San Francisco   Lisbon   London
Madrid   Mexico City   Milan   New Delhi   San Juan   Seoul
Singapore   Sydney   Toronto

The McGraw·Hill Companies

1 2 3 4 5 6 7 8 9 0   DOC/DOC   1 6 5 4 3 2 1

ISBN: 978-0-07-175451-4 (print book)
MHID: 0-07-175451-2

ISBN: 978-0-07-176014-0 (e-book)
MHID: 0-07-176014-8

Library of Congress Cataloging-in-Publication Data
Abraham, Joe.
   Entrepreneurial DNA : the breakthrough discovery that aligns your business to your unique strengths / by Joe Abraham.
       p. cm.
   ISBN 978-0-07-175451-4 (hardback)
   1. Success in business—Psychological aspects.   2. Entrepreneurship.
3. Businesspeople—Psychology.   4. Business planning. I. Title.
   HF5386.A4234 2011
   658.4'21—dc22

                                                            2010052799

McGraw-Hill books are available at special quantity discounts to use as premiums and sales promotions or for use in corporate training programs. To contact a representative, please e-mail us at bulksales@mcgraw-hill.com.

This book is printed on acid-free paper.

I'd like to dedicate this book to my boys, JJ and Zach.
Here's hoping the entrepreneurial bug bites you too someday.

contents

acknowledgments

To my awesome wife and best friend Sally, thank you for your unconditional love, patience and care as I went through my entrepreneurial journey. You've been my greatest cheerleader and inspiration and I thank God for giving me the gift of *you*. To mom and dad, thank you for your loving support and favor as I negotiated the ups and downs of the journey.

To my agent Cynthia Zigmund and the team at Literary Services, Inc., thank you for believing in this first-time author and putting your name on the line to bring it to such a fantastic publisher. Your insight, input and candid feedback during the proposal stage were mission critical to this book project becoming a reality.

To Knox Huston my brilliant editor, thank you for the passion with which you sold this project to the team at McGraw Hill Professional. I am also indebted to you for guiding me through the editing process and adding your incredible talent to the output of this book. Entrepreneurial DNA would not be what it is today without your contributions. Sara Hendricksen at McGraw Hill—you rock. I would also like to thank McGraw-Hill production editor Scott Kurtz and copy editor Nina Levy Girard for your outstanding work.

Special appreciation goes to my friend Garry Arasmith who was BOSI's biggest proponent right after the discovery. Thanks G for not letting me shelf the concept like I kept trying to do. Your persistent commitment to see BOSI impact businesses around the world was a key driver to me sitting down and working on the book manuscript.

Steve Thompson, thank you for believing in me and this project long before there was a measurable reason to do so. Rob Armstrong, you da man. The Opportunist in you kept me fired up and "tank full" even when the reality said otherwise. Trey Morris, your friendship and partnership have been of immeasurable value. We've got a great journey ahead of us. Lukas Naugle, my brand and content strategist--you are the bat that breaks any box I put myself in. Thank you for that.

Last but by no means the least, to my mentors, business partners, and clients, thank you for allowing me into your businesses and lives. There's a part of every single one of you in this book. From the highest highs to the lowest lows we have shared together, we learned lessons about business and entrepreneurial life that are now encapsulated in this work. I hope you are proud to know that your story now stands to impact the lives and businesses of entrepreneurs around the world.

introduction

I vividly remember the experience of watching my first-ever television show. It was the late 1970s in New Delhi, India. Dad didn't see the point of us owning a TV, given that there was one national channel that delivered a few hours of fuzzy programming each evening. Our neighbors, however, had just bought a brand-new TV and invited me and my sisters to come over on a Wednesday night to watch an "American" show with them.

I was just beside myself in excitement. Not only was I going to get to see what a TV looked like, I was going to get my first real taste of America! I don't think I slept very well the night before. I remember tossing and turning in glee, just hoping and praying for daybreak so I could begin the official countdown to that coveted experience.

The day of the event, I remember bragging to my friends at school and on the playground about my elite invitation for later that night. By the time 8 p.m. arrived on the clock, I was bouncing off the walls. No sooner did my mom give us the okay to walk politely over to the neighbor's house, than I was pounding on their door, begging to be let in. A few minutes later, we were sitting cross-legged on a beautiful Persian rug, ready to take in the entire experience. "Who cares about the food and drink?" I remember thinking to myself, "Let's get this amazing device turned on!"

When the lady of the house finally walked over to turn the unit on, my heart skipped a beat. A few seconds of snowy fuzz eventually gave way to the breathtaking black-and-white footage of Lucy and Ricky Ricardo bantering back and forth on the *I Love Lucy* show.

I was in awe. Instantly I was transported to Lucy and Ricky's living room and kitchen thousands of miles away. It felt like I was right there with them.

That was a big night for me. I had experienced something amazing out of a 13-inch black-and-white screen. "This is the most incredible thing ever," I thought to myself. "I can't imagine anything better than this."

You and I now have the luxury of knowing that a 13-inch black-and-white TV with rabbit-ear antenna was not the end of TV innovation. Today as I pen the words on this page, my six-year-old is nagging me about the latest 3-D High Definition television that we absolutely *have* to own.

"Really? A high definition TV in *3-D?*" I asked him. "Oh yeah, Dad. It's as thin as your computer screen and you put on these special glasses, and the stuff feels like it's coming out of the TV right on top of you," he replied.

Things change so fast, don't they? Black-and-white TV seems like the dark ages now.

I hope you'll feel the same way about *old-school entrepreneurship* once you are done with this book.

Here's why.

For centuries, entrepreneurs have been put in one big box. We have been told that we are all the same. That is the single biggest misconception in entrepreneurship—the one-size-fits-all approach to business startup, growth, and exit. Since we were assumed to all be the *same* (kind of like the borg in *Star Trek*), it was assumed that we should all have the same modus operandi in business and life.

In *old-school* entrepreneurship, Donald Trump, Sir Richard Branson, and Gary Vaynerchuk weren't different from you—they were a *better version* of you.

In *old school* entrepreneurship, if you didn't work an insane amount of hours, love marketing, selling, negotiating, and firing people, you were the inferior version of the genuine article.

In *old school* entrepreneurship, if an idea worked for someone else and it didn't work for you, you were the one with a big "L for loser" on your forehead.

I find it interesting that entrepreneurship—the source of every great innovation—has not experienced any true innovation of its own. We have been operating with a century-old playbook, a playbook that is the equivalent of that 13-inch black-and-white TV I first watched Lucy and Ricky on.

Sitting cross-legged on that Persian rug that night, I thought things could never get better than black-and-white television. After all, Lucy and Ricky looked and sounded great. At least, that's what I thought, given the paradigm in which I was living.

I want to give kudos to the folks who built the first black-and-white TV. They did an amazing thing. Without them, my kid wouldn't have a reason to drag me to the gadget store to buy a 3-D HDTV. The same is true of the good folks who have written books and taught classes on old-school entrepreneurship to date. They paved the way for what you and I are about to learn together now.

But it is time to move on.

The old-school, one-size-fits-all, black-and-white version needs to be archived in a museum somewhere. Instead, there is a whole new way for you and me to look at entrepreneurship. It is a whole new paradigm for how we can live and operate as entrepreneurs. I want to invite you to experience this next generation of entrepreneurship in its *multidimensional, rich, color, high fidelity coolness.*

In our short time together, I plan to introduce you to a game-changing paradigm in the world of entrepreneurship called Entrepreneurial DNA. In the first part of this book, you and I are going to focus on what I call the Discover process. The Discover process is all about you figuring out what type of entrepreneur you really are. You'll learn about the tendencies, predispositions, strengths, and weaknesses of your unique entrepreneurial DNA (also called your BOSI Profile).

Next, we'll dive into the Design Process. The Design Process is all about you taking what you have learned and crafting a breakthrough strategic plan for your business that (for the first time) is built around your unique gifting.

Finally, we'll talk about the Deploy Process. This is where the rubber hits the road and you execute your breakthrough strategic plan into the marketplace.

I hope you are ready (for the breakthrough) and willing (to pull the trigger) to see what the next generation of entrepreneurship is all about.

part one

What Is My Entrepreneurial DNA?

The saying goes, "Your mind is like an umbrella—it only works when it is open." With that said, the only thing I am going to ask of you at this point is that you keep an open mind as you get into the first few chapters of this book. What you are about to learn has never been talked about before (although you've intuitively thought about this topic quite often).

So strap yourself in and let's kick off this magic carpet ride together. We are going to begin the journey by discovering your entrepreneurial DNA. It is a fun process that will instantly drive you to start comparing your profile to that of your peers.

Have fun, and may you never be the same!

chapter

1

Four Entrepreneurs
Walk into a Bar . . .

Thursday, 8:47 p.m. Westin DFW Hotel–Dallas, Texas

After a long day of glad-handing, power meetings, and vendor interviews at the Franchise Expo Show, Bob Morris strolls into the lobby bar area for his last meeting of the night. Earlier that day, he had met Sue Thomas, a CPA who was a featured presenter at the event. Bob was so impressed with Sue's presentation on *10 Strategies to Improve Your Bottom Line*, he just had to meet Sue and see what it would take to hire her as his accountant and financial advisor. Bob had approached Sue immediately after her presentation and asked to schedule the meeting. Sue obliged and they decided that the hotel lobby bar area would be the ideal meeting place right after their already scheduled dinner meetings.

As Bob walked up to Sue, he noticed that she was already in conversation with two other people wearing attendee name badges. To Sue's left was Omar Kelly. According to Omar's name badge, he was representing Success Ventures Inc. To Sue's right was Ingrid Fuller, owner of Ginoma Life Sciences. As Bob neared the group, Sue was quick to recognize him and introduce him around. Since Bob and Sue's meeting wasn't scheduled to begin for another 15 minutes or so, the four new acquaintances—Bob, Sue, Ingrid, and Omar—kept the pleasantries going.

"So Bob, what do you do for a living?" Omar asked.

"I own Pizza Pete's," Bob replied.

"You mean you own a Pizza Pete's franchise?" Omar questioned. "I stopped at their booth earlier today and was very interested in them. It sounds like they are having a ton of growth."

"Actually, I own the entire Pizza Pete's franchise," said Bob. "My college buddy and I started the company 15 years ago and I bought him out about five years back. So now I'm the guy who gets to write and cash all the checks!" He said with a big grin on his face.

Omar was beside himself. He was standing next to a multi-millionaire. As Omar was listening to Bob talk, he couldn't help notice Bob's $2,000 suit, alligator-skin shoes, and French cuff shirt barely exposing what looked like a Rolex Presidential. Omar's heart rate climbed just a notch or two. See, Omar was a huge fan of success. As a matter of fact, he had named his company Success Ventures Inc. for that very reason. His dream was to be a business mogul. He could see the future in his mind's eye as clear as the day itself. Success Ventures Inc. would someday be the holding company for various business interests generating huge sums of cash each month. It would provide him the lifestyle he had always dreamed of. One of the reasons Omar had attended the Franchise Expo Show in Dallas today was to find a ground-floor business opportunity he could sink his teeth into and parlay into his first big win. Needless to say, Omar was pretty fired up to be standing next to a guy like Bob—a guy who could give Omar an inside track to the next ground-floor opportunity within the Pizza Pete's franchise. Omar asked question after question about Bob's company, success, and lifestyle. He was in hog heaven.

Interestingly enough, Bob didn't seem to mind the questions at all. After all, he had worked his tail off to build Pizza Pete's into a

$40-million franchise organization. He was about to turn the corner after some legal battles to open up enough territories to take the company to over $200 million in sales. Bob bragged on and on about his exploits while Omar's mental computer burned gigabyte after gigabyte of audio and video content into its memory.

As Sue heard Bob talk about his enterprise, she was getting excited as well. After all, the reason Sue went out and did speaking gigs like the one she had done earlier in the day was to establish herself as an expert in corporate finance. Her whole angle was to have CEOs like Bob see her speak in front of a large audience and then pursue her to hire her as a consultant or an advisor. She quietly listened to Bob and Omar banter back and forth waiting for the moment when Bob would turn to her and say, "Oh by the way Sue, I was so impressed with your presentation today, that I want you to come in and help Pizza Pete's during our next phase of growth." That would be music to Sue's ears.

About 15 minutes into the conversation, Bob noticed that Ingrid hadn't said a whole lot since the start. In his desire to engage Ingrid as part of the conversation, he said, "So Ingrid, what brought you to the Expo today?"

"Oh, I just came because Sue was speaking today. I usually don't attend seminars and expos like this," she said. "I'm just a science geek, and not that interested in actually running a business. My motivation is doing good for others."

"A science geek, what do you mean?" Bob asked. "And what is Ginoma Life Sciences all about?"

Ingrid went on to sheepishly explain how she had stumbled across a supplemental digestive enzyme while doing research on an ailment her daughter had at a very young age. The discovery of this supplemental enzyme is what saved her daughter's life. But it didn't stop there. Doctors from around the world began to contact Ingrid looking for information about the product that had helped her daughter so much.

Ingrid openly admitted to Bob, Sue, and Omar that she really had no intent to start a company like Ginoma Life Sciences. She was just doing something she loved and a business has blossomed up around her.

"You mean you didn't write a business plan and find investors first?" Omar asked in bewilderment.

"No." Ingrid replied. "Like I said, I really didn't want to be a businessperson. I'm just a mom. But thanks to people like Sue, who watch over the finances, and my husband Bill, who runs the business itself, the business just keeps growing. Personally, I don't get involved with how much our product costs or how to read the financial statements that Sue sends us every month."

"This is so unfair!" Omar thought to himself. After all, he had invested countless hours and tens of thousands of dollars researching business ventures, setting business goals, attending business seminars, and going through coaching. He had already invested in several ground-floor opportunities with varying results—mostly painful. And here was Ingrid, with no training or desire to even own a business—way ahead of the game on her first venture.

Sue was taking it all in. She was happy that Ingrid has given her such a glowing review. That had to score major points toward Bob hiring her. The less Sue had to say to "sell" herself, the better. She wanted to be the expert everyone came to. She didn't want to be the overly eager "used-car salesman" that Omar appeared to be. As much as she appreciated him being part of the conversation, she wished Omar would just go away. But then she saw how much Bob seemed to like Omar and she thought "well, if it keeps Bob happy for now, I'll just grin and bear the fact that Omar is here."

It was 9:24 p.m. now and Bob was just getting started. He painted a grand picture for Omar of where Pizza Pete's was going in the future and how Omar could be part of it. Every once in a while, he'd stop to give Ingrid a business tip. Every time Bob would turn to give her a tip, Ingrid would just shrug and say, "I could never do what you do. Thankfully, I'm fortunate enough to have a support team like my husband and Sue to handle those things for me."

Freeze Frame

Have you started to pick up on the differences within this four-some yet? My guess is that you have. But just to make sure, let's listen in to one last interaction amongst the group before Sue and Bob break away for their overdue meeting.

Press Play

Sensing that their time together was coming to the end, Omar jumped in to ask a question that had been nagging at him all night. "Let me ask this question of all of you. It's a question my success coach asked me. I'd like to hear each of your answers."

"Why did you go into business and what do you want from your business?" "Oh that's easy." Bob said. "I'll go first."

"I went into business for myself because building business is what I've always done and I do it well. Even after I sell Pizza Pete's for a couple of hundred million, I'll probably start another company. Maybe next time, I'll take on Google!" He chuckled.

Sue was next. "I went into business to be my own boss. I was working with a Fortune 500 accounting firm, but after the long commute and 80-hour work weeks, I decided that running my own boutique accounting firm would give me the quality of life and income I wanted. So far, it has worked out great. I'll be doing this for a long time!"

"You already know my answer Omar." Ingrid said as she smiled. "I really had no plans to own a business. It just happened. At the end of the day, I don't really care if I make a lot of money or sell the business for the kind of money Bob just talked about. I'm just happy to know that the product that saved my baby's life is helping other people."

Bob let out a big sigh as he heard Ingrid's answer. "What a waste!" He thought to himself. "Ingrid has a billion-dollar product that should be on the shelves of every Walmart and Walgreens and she's tinkering around with a homemade label printer and a garage full of product."

"Well, thanks to all of you for sharing your answers." Omar said. "Just so you know, I went into business to get rich." But that wasn't all Omar had to say. "I want to find business ventures that are positioned for explosive growth, get in on the ground floor, and ride the wave all the way to the top. Once I've done that a few times in a few different industries, Success Ventures Inc. will have a huge amount of cash flow coming in every month. I'll have no employees—except maybe an assistant. I'll spend a few minutes each morning checking my portfolios and doing some trading. Then I'll be off to the golf course with my buddies and enjoy the rest of the day with friends and family. To me, that's what being a businessman is all about."

Sue was ready to give Omar an earful. She couldn't disagree more with Omar on the issue. But she noticed that Bob had just glanced at his watch. It was time for Bob and Sue to have their private meeting. It was time for Bob to offer Sue the consulting gig she had worked so hard to position herself for.

Ingrid was tired. She wasn't used to such business-intensive days and late nights. She told everyone goodnight and excused herself to her hotel room.

Omar smiled with glee as Bob handed him his business card and wrote his cell phone number on it. "Give me a call, Omar. You and I can make a ton of money together. With your attitude and my expertise, the sky is the limit my friend," he said.

Sue gave Omar a firm handshake and promised Ingrid they'd see each other at the breakfast buffet the next morning.

Does One Size Fit All?

I'm asking that question rhetorically for now. I just want you to think about it as we go through the next few pages in this book. Are the four characters in our lobby bar scene really the same? Should all four be put in one generic "entrepreneur" pigeonhole and told to follow the same strategy in business as the next person? Are Bob and Ingrid really wired to operate in business the same way? How about Sue and Omar?

chapter

2

Your Entrepreneurial DNA Drives Your Business Strategy

Maybe It's Just Me!

I am sure you have found yourself in the same position I have. Arms thrown up in the air questioning how the entrepreneur next door pulled off a feat you couldn't. What is really frustrating is when it appears as though he or she spent *half* the energy getting it done. Maybe it was a marketing campaign or a product launch. It could have been a sales strategy or a hiring decision. The bottom line is that he or she did it better and/or faster than you could have. When things like that happen, you find yourself saying, "Maybe it's just me."

Maybe It's Just Your Type

You probably have some history with dogs. You either have one, or grew up with one, or saw your neighbor with one. When you see a dog, you instantly recognize it as a dog. Because dogs are dogs, right? Generally, they have ears and good hearing, a nose with an acute sense of smell, four legs, and fur. They run, they play, they bark, and they leave land mines on the lawn.

Some breeds, though, are specifically bred based on their natural gifts. Think about the genetic and phenotypic differences in these breeds. Imagine being a basset hound taking on a greyhound in a sprint to the finish line. Imagine being a golden retriever going head-to-head against a pit bull in a job interview for "scary guard dog."

Even playing field? I don't think so.

It's just the same with people. We share some characteristics, but each of us has a unique and distinct makeup. When it comes to entrepreneurship, some of us are "purebreds" and carry a distinct set of characteristics and gifts. Others of us are "mutts" who have a blend of various strengths and weaknesses.

But, read any book on entrepreneurship and the authors will say the same thing. "You are an entrepreneur—so here is the silver bullet on how to become a better _____" (fill in the blank with marketer, leader, communicator, negotiator, candlestick maker).

Attend any seminar for entrepreneurs and the speakers will say essentially the same thing. Hire an expert to write your business plan, design a go-to-market strategy, or generate online traffic, and the same anthem will start to play.

However, these "gurus" are all making the same fatal assumption that you are like *every* other entrepreneur out there. Think about any popular program you've seen out there. It usually has the founder's name built into the title like "Tom's Selling," "Barb's Branding," or "Tim's Negotiating." Essentially what they are selling is this:

1. "I figured out a way to become successful in _____ (selling, branding, negotiating, Internet marketing, flipping real estate, etc.)."
2. "I took my step-by-step action plan and success blueprint and put it into my _____ (home-study, live seminar, online membership) program."

3. "Now you can have the *exact* same success I had if you *just* follow my system."

Really, guru? Really? I can't blame the gurus for doing it. That's how we were all taught in the classroom of *old school* entrepreneurship. As a matter of fact, I built a couple of training companies having made a very similar "you can do it if I did it" claim. The old-fashioned notion was that what worked for the entrepreneur next door would also work for *you*. But you know from experience that isn't always true. Just as our four characters from Chapter 1, you know that you are not built to do the things *every* other entrepreneur does. On the flip side, you've probably noticed others try to duplicate some of your best practices only to fall flat on their faces.

You have strengths, weaknesses, and tendencies that give you a *distinct* modus operandi.

- Maybe you are the person who has thousands of people following you on Twitter or maybe you are struggling to get follower no. 58.
- Maybe you are the one that has the gift to build and nurture long-term interpersonal relationships or maybe you are the type that rips through people faster than a tornado in Wichita, Kansas.
- Maybe you are an entrepreneur who finds marketing and lead generation as easy as flipping on a light switch or maybe you are someone who finds it harder than pushing a bowling ball through a garden hose.
- Maybe you are one of those who starts a business and runs it for 20-plus years, or maybe you are one of those who jumps from business opportunity to business opportunity like a frog hopping lily pads on a pond.

Here's my point. You can't be *all* of the above. The black-and-white, old school version of entrepreneurship assumed you *were* all of the above. It assumed that you would walk up to the buffet of business strategy—try a little of everything—and through trial and error, find what works for you.

How's that going for you? It sure didn't go well for me.

You Have an Entrepreneurial DNA That Drives You

When it comes to your health, you have genes that drive your predisposition to wellness or disease. There is a genetic code that sets a foundation for who you *are*. Knowing your genetic predisposition empowers you to make lifestyle and environmental decisions to improve or worsen your health. For example, your doctor can look at your medical history and the results from a series of tests and help you map out a plan for recovery from an ailment. A nutritionist or personal trainer can help you figure out a meal and exercise plan. A chiropractor or naturopath can help you put together a wellness initiative. The point here is that each of these experts must run a series of tests to figure out who you are *before* making recommendations on what you should (or should not) do.

Your Entrepreneurial DNA is no different. You have a unique set of traits prebuilt into your brain. That DNA telegraphs your *potential* strengths, weaknesses, and tendencies. Being aware of that DNA will allow you to sit down by yourself, or with an expert, to map out a plan for your business that is perfectly suited for you. It will also allow you to recognize when you are in your sweet spot of giftedness and when you are in the danger zone of trying to be someone you are not. That's why the first thing you and I are going to do together is discover your unique Entrepreneurial DNA.

Why It's Important to Discover Your Entrepreneurial DNA

In 2005, I was introduced to an entrepreneur named Kendal Yonomoto. Kendal is a former Canadian pro tour golfer. Since he left the tour, he became a student of wellness and started an innovative business that combined golf skills with conditioning and fitness. He travels all over the world doing his golf conditioning program in partnership with top golf pros.

Kendal got his hands on an OmegaWave, a piece of diagnostic equipment used by many professional teams and Olympic organizations. Its purpose is to run a diagnostic on an athlete to give the trainer insight on how best to build the day's workout plan.

While demonstrating the system for me, Kendal said, "We have learned much more about this device since we have been using it. We are at the point where the data literally tells us if someone has the *profile* of a super athlete."

In bewilderment, I asked what he meant.

I could run this test on an 8-year-old, for example, and I could tell you if he has the genetics and the predisposition to be a star athlete," he said.

The capitalist in me could not contain itself. "Imagine what a parent would pay to have his kid tested *before* spending tens of thousands of dollars in classes, coaches, and team fees!"

I volunteered to be a guinea pig. I was really curious as how the system would profile me (a former athlete and now a weekend warrior).

While I was lying there, with all the electrodes on me, Kendal asked, "So, what do you do to work out, Joe? Give me some insight so I can tell you where you are at."

I recall telling him about my fairly infrequent and painful visits to the gym. I told him about my love for playing soccer. Soccer was, and is, my primary form of exercise. Then we chatted about a few other things until the test was done.

His laptop fired off the test results. Kendal looked at them, and the first thing he said was, "Joe, you *don't have the profile* for a soccer player. You should not be playing competitive soccer."

My jaw fell to the floor. How dare he say that!

"What do you mean I'm not a soccer player?" I sputtered.

"Look at your *profile*," Kendal said, showing me. "You are built more as a football player than a soccer player. Soccer players are endurance athletes. They are called on to sustain sprints and recover very quickly to repeat that process 50 to 60 times in a game. Your *profile*, everything from your VO$_2$ max to your fast twitch muscle, characteristics suggest you would have been a better football player where you go in for a play and then come off the field. Bursts of activity, not continued, ongoing activity."

As I thought about it, it made sense. "You know what?" I thought. "That's one of the reasons why there are several times during a soccer game where I get completely outplayed. I see an opportunity to make a play, but someone with better capacity than me beats me to the punch." My capacity to play flag football, however, was quite different.

Here's why this story applies to you as an entrepreneur. A lot of entrepreneurs think they are "soccer players" in the world of business. So they step out on to the field and try to engage in an activity they *think* they are good at, even though results would say otherwise. That's dangerous.

They think, "I'm going to use social media just like Bill did to get a huge market position." Or, "I'm going to do my own sales and marketing." Or, "I'll start this new company and build it up to a billion dollars." Maybe. But maybe you're not built for that!

You can force yourself. You can even love it. You can go out there and try to do it, but it's going to be a lot more work, and you may not even succeed. You are going to be competing against people who are more gifted "soccer players." It's going to be easier for them. They will be in their sweet spot of giftedness, and have a competition-crushing market advantage.

"But my business is doing great!" you may say. "We're doing millions in sales, we dominate our market, everyone is paid handsomely. . ."

Okay, I'm happy to hear that. How's your *life* doing?

Are you in balance? Are you and your spouse growing and thriving in your marriage? Are you spending quality, uninterrupted time with your children every day? How is your spiritual walk doing? How's your health?

Listen, if the sun is shining on the beaches of your business *and* your life, and everything is in perfect harmony, then you have intuitively figured this whole DNA thing out. For the rest of us, there's this book.

The whole intent of this process is for you as an entrepreneur to say, "Maybe, just maybe, I am a football player who is trying to act like a soccer player." Discovering your Entrepreneurial DNA will give you the freedom to excel in areas in which you are gifted. You'll leverage your strengths to gain market position. However, you'll also give yourself permission to say no in other areas. You'll thankfully release the death grip on the steering wheel of *some* areas of your business and reap the benefits of doing so.

But just to make sure we get past rhetoric and instead talk specifics, let's take a look at some real-life scenarios in which Entrepreneurial DNA plays itself out.

[chapter]

3

Entrepreneurial DNA
in Action

I want to take an opportunity to show you how Entrepreneurial DNA plays out in real-life situations. In this chapter, we're going to take a look at three real-life situations I have plucked out of my memory banks. Each of these situations really did happen. I was part of every one of them. They represent some of the most common situations in which Entrepreneurial DNA is the deciding factor between success and failure. As you read through these situations, I hope you'll start to get a grasp of how important your Entrepreneurial DNA truly is.

How Entrepreneurial DNA Affects Business Selection

Alex had spent over 20 years in the Telecom industry. His most recent jaunt was with Lucent Technologies, where he was a senior project manager. With that post came a ton of responsibility. Alex was the guy who was brought in to manage highly complex project deployments with hundreds (sometimes thousands) of moving parts and interdependencies. Alex handled the projects like a pro. He quickly became the go-to guy for most of the sales organization. "I want Alex to run my project once it is sold," the sales guys would say. "I've already pitched him as part of the project to the client."

Needless to say, Alex was brimming with confidence. He was good at what he did. People counted on him everyday to do an excellent job. And he did.

But there was a part of Alex that had gotten bored of the routine at Lucent. Project in, project out—it was all getting a bit predictable. He was making great money and his 401-k was growing at a pretty fast clip. But Alex was feeling underutilized. He was getting antsy for something bigger and better.

Alex was surprisingly happy when his boss called him into the office one day to let him know that due to some restructuring Alex had the choice of relocating to keep his current post or taking an early retirement package.

"Well, this is not what I expected," Alex thought to himself. "But I'm actually glad this is happening."

It didn't take long for Alex and his wife Gina to come to terms with the fact that relocation was not an option, so he took the package. Almost overnight, Alex went from being an employee at a global powerhouse to being retired with a bagful of money—looking for something to do.

"I'm not going back to work at another big company. That's for sure," Alex said to Gina at the kitchen table. "I'm just tired of the rat race."

"Why don't we start that business we've always talked about starting?" Gina asked encouragingly. "We've got some money in the bank. You are amazing at getting things pulled together and working. I can support you with any marketing and promotions for the business. We could be our own boss, call our own shots, and you won't have to answer to anyone ever again."

The prospect of being CEO of a highly successful business did appeal to Alex. His wife's confidence in him made the movie playing in his mind even better. "Let's do it," he exclaimed. "Let's do it."

The Purchase

Alex had loved cars all his life. He loved driving them, fixing them, reading about them, and talking about them. He was always envious of car dealers who got to walk on the lot of their dealership each morning and have the "pick of the litter" when it came to choosing which car they would drive that day.

"Imagine being able to drive any car you want for as long as you want. Then when you get bored, just park that car and pick up another one. That would be a great life," he thought.

The idea of owning a dealership bustling with good-looking salespeople, happy customers, and rave reviews really appealed to Alex. Gina was excited about it as well. After all, she could put her 15-year history in marketing promotions to work and make sure that the phone never stopped ringing.

So the search began and it didn't take long to find a very attractive opportunity. Sitting right at the intersection of two very busy county highways was a truck dealership with a motivated seller. But this wasn't just any ordinary business opportunity. The dealership had been there for over 20 years. It had a stellar reputation across the region. Did I mention that the busy highway happened to be the only thoroughfare connecting a remote town in New Hampshire to the Boston area? It was a target-rich environment of commuters. The value of the real estate itself was almost worth the seller's asking price.

"It's not a car dealership, but the price is right," Alex said to Gina. "We can always expand the lot and add used cars." There were two service bays that Alex was really excited about. He imagined himself with his hands full of grease every day, fixing cars and trucks for his fanatical customers. What could be better? It certainly was a far cry from sitting in a cubicle messing around with project management software.

The negotiations went quickly. The seller was motivated. Amidst the negotiations, Alex agreed to keep a couple of key employees on the payroll as a favor to the seller. The business had done $4 million in the previous year and almost $7 million the year before. Alex and Gina were excited. With Alex's ability to get things done and Gina's marketing background, they would have the dealership back to $7 million in no time and on its way to $10 million within a few months. Or so they thought.

The purchase price ended up being a bit more than they originally expected. Gina and Alex had to borrow some of the funds from their parents. Half a million dollars to be exact. After the bank extended them a couple of loans, totaling just over $700,000, they became the proud owners of a great little truck dealership.

The first few months in business were pretty exciting for Alex and Gina. They pulled into the parking lot of their dealership and surveyed their property and assets with pride. The phone would ring every day. Customers would come in for repairs and parts almost like clockwork.

By the tail end of their first year in business, some challenges began to emerge. The two sales guys they had inherited from the previous owner were deadweight as far as Alex was concerned. They didn't work hard and they complained a ton. They sat there waiting for the phone to ring. When the phone did ring, they would chit-chat with the wrong customers and mess up the deals with the right ones. Alex had had enough. He didn't feel comfortable firing the guys. After all, they were nice guys and it was good to have a couple of sales guys in the showroom so people didn't think this was a mom-and-pop operation. But just to make sure the cash register rang, Alex decided that he was best suited on the front lines selling. After all, *who better to get the company back to $7 million in sales than the owner himself* right?

"Truck buyers are funny that way," Alex said to Gina. "They always want to talk to the owner to get the deal done. So why have a salesperson in the middle who we pay 25 percent of the net sale to when the customer wants to talk to me anyway?"

Freeze Frame

In the upcoming chapters of this book, we are going to learn that Entrepreneurial DNA is our modus operandi in business. It's the voices in our head that drive the decisions we make. Every time we make a decision, our Entrepreneurial DNA is at work influencing those choices. Alex's Entrepreneurial DNA is in action right now. During his career at Lucent, he would never allow an unseasoned sales person to be assigned to the task of growing his business. In his previous life, he would have demanded a highly qualified expert. However, when given the title of *business owner*, he is making a very different set of choices—driven by a very different decision matrix.

It is important to point out that Alex had no formal sales training. He was a certified project manager. We'll learn later in this book that there is a certain Entrepreneurial DNA that is gifted to sell and promote. Alex didn't know this at the time, but he had little-to-none of that DNA in him.

Gina—with 15 years of marketing under her belt—was spending 80 percent of her day operating dealer management software, building accounting spreadsheets, ordering supplies, and running payroll. She was far outside her comfort zone or skill set. But she was a *business owner* now and had to do whatever was needed to keep the business going.

The phone was still ringing and customers were still pulling into the parking lot to look at trucks, so Alex and Gina kept on keeping on. The perception was that things were moving in the right direction.

Push Play

At the end of their first full year in business, when the CPA presented the financials, it was a shock to both Alex and Gina. "What do you mean we only did $2.2 million this year? We've been busier than we have ever been in our lives!" Alex ranted.

"You're going to need to set up a new line of credit with the bank," the CPA said. "You are running too close to breakeven and you need some cushion to buy inventory and make payroll on time."

When I was introduced to Alex and Gina, they were in their third year of operating the dealership. The phone wasn't ringing as much—and when it did ring, it was a tire kicker or a price shopper. The stock market crash of 2008 had sent most new truck buyers running for cover. Alex found himself spending four to five times as much time working the same types of deals as just a couple of years before. And yet, most of the deals were falling apart at the last minute. Alex was extremely frustrated. It showed in his attitude and in his results. Customers could see this from a mile away. So they kept low-balling him.

Revenues had dropped steadily for the three-year window and the couple had infused an additional $400,000 into the business from a home equity line of credit. The debt service on the business was crushing to say the least. The couple had lots of ideas they wanted to implement—ideas that could generate great results. But three years into a tailspin, they were tired, overwhelmed, and somewhat petrified of making another bad decision.

"What makes me think that after all these dumb decisions I have been making for three years that I am suddenly going to make a good one?" Alex said with a commanding voice over the phone to me. "I could borrow another $100,000 to put into this business and flush it down the toilet for all intents and purposes.

"I own a business I apparently had no business owning. We are close to $2 million in debt to banks and family. These prospects don't know a good deal if it hits them in the forehead—and we're losing $40,000 a month," he said.

Three years into his painful and frustrating journey, Alex had intuitively figured out what you are about to learn in the pages of this book. Not everyone is built to be a car dealer. Not everyone has the DNA to build and manage a commissioned sales force. Just because you like something (like cars and trucks), doesn't necessarily make you the ideal candidate to own a business that sells and services it.

How Entrepreneurial DNA Drives a Quest to Duplicate Success

James had been a salesman all his life. As a kid, he was the one on the schoolyard making up wild stories of how his dad was an astronaut and how James himself was going to be going to the moon with NASA on their next expedition. He was so convincing in his delivery that even his teacher had to do a double take and check out his stories.

James was also entrepreneurial at heart. He was the kid with the lemonade stand at age 7. He made his stand more competitive by adding cookies and ice cream for sale. Long before eBay opened its doors, James was running a baseball card buying-and-trading platform out of his basement for friends. He also had somewhat of an addictive personality. When he latched onto something, he dove in hook, line, and sinker. He didn't just play soccer, he obsessed on soccer to the point of driving himself to be the best in town. By the time he was in high school, he was part of a travel team invited to tour in Germany and play against some of the best teams in Europe.

By the time he was 20 years old, he met a successful entrepreneur who was just getting started building a direct-response marketing company. This successful entrepreneur took such a liking to James and his youthful energy, he took James under his wing and committed to teach him everything he knew.

The timing could not have been better for James. His new mentor was on a rocket ship of success. The company went from zero to over $50 million in sales in just a few years. James got to come along for the ride. By the time he was age 23, James was making a six-figure income. By the time he was age 25, he was appointed executive vice president of his mentor's company. He was overseeing tens of millions of dollars a year in revenues and learning a ton about running a high-growth company. His confidence was brimming. Then the inevitable happened. *The student became smarter than the teacher.*

After a few heated arguments about the way things "should be," it became more apparent that it was time for the mentor and the apprentice to part ways. James was convinced that he was smarter and better equipped to build a better version of his mentor's company. He maneuvered his way into some income streams that belonged to his mentor and used that as his seed capital to start his first venture.

Remember, James was a dynamic fellow. He was a charismatic promoter since his days on the schoolyard. It was easy for him to paint a blue-sky picture to employees, customers, and investors. His first company took off pretty well. Within months, he was clearing $10,000 to $30,000 a month in personal income. Not bad for a guy in his early thirties. He could have sat back and kept things moving at a steady pace, but something inside James wasn't satisfied with "average" results. He wanted "extraordinary" results. What he really wanted was to outdo his former mentor. That was the big monkey on his back.

When a high-growth, high-risk opportunity presented itself to James, he had a hard time saying no. After all, if just one of those opportunities panned out, he'd be set for life. More importantly, his mentor would have to admit defeat and crown James as the better and smarter businessman.

But, three years into his solo-entrepreneur journey, James had multiple ventures up and running. He was so distracted putting out fires in the new ventures that his core business began to suffer. Cash-flow management became a real nightmare. He was pulling cash out of his core business to fund fledgling ventures he had started up or invested in. It wasn't long before even his most loyal clients in the core business began to sense it was time to move on.

James's frustration grew on a daily basis. How did his mentor build his company to over $50 million in just a couple of years? After all, James was there for every waking moment of the journey. And here he was, implementing his mentor's playbook almost to a "T" and the walls were crumbling around him.

It drove James almost insane when he would hear from friends he had in common with his mentor that his mentor was now expanding internationally and generating hundreds of millions in revenues in other countries. Meanwhile, James was struggling to make payroll for his staff of 20 employees.

What in the world was going on? It didn't make any sense to James. He was smarter than his former boss. He certainly had the advantage of having learned everything he needed to know before setting out on his own. He had followed the game plan. But he was failing.

Freeze Frame

I wonder if this is exactly how my beagle would feel if he had to engage in a guard dog contest with a pit bull. Don't get me wrong. My beagle is outstanding at sounding his beagle howl when anyone gets within 50 yards of our house. In that sense, he is serving the role of a "guard dog." But a savvy dog person simply needs to look at my beagle to know that he's not really a guard dog; he's a "scared-alert" dog. The closer someone gets to him, the farther he backs away. By the time the visitor gets to the garage area, my beagle is wagging his tail and sniffing around. I don't think that even the savviest dog person would dare take the same chance with a barking pit bull.

James needed to just look back on his life and recognize the signs. He was a gifted promoter and a master salesman. That didn't mean he was just as gifted as a business operator. James was highly successful within the confines of an established business. But did that really mean he would be just as successful out on his own? His obsessive-and-addictive nature could be harnessed to build a huge company (most big company leaders have that trait). However, his inability to focus on his core business and his desire to get rich faster than normal were impeding his success.

Push Play

When James hit rock bottom, he wasn't alone. Many of his employees got hurt in the process. Some of his employees had become so enamored with James's blue-sky vision that they had become investors and cosigners with James. When his companies failed, they all failed within months of each other. People all around James lost hundreds of thousands of dollars in personal wealth.

James had fallen victim to one of the biggest culprits in the world of business. He was chasing the success of someone who was built very differently than he was. But nobody told James that. He was a victim of old-school entrepreneurship where *if it worked for his mentor, it would work for him.*

How Entrepreneurial DNA Affects Company Leadership

If he were to take an inventory of his worldly possessions, Harry would certainly qualify as "having it all." Over 20 years, he had built his company to become the largest maker of specialty foods in Europe. With sales of over 20 million and a 20 percent bottom line, life was good.

Harry's state-of-the-art factory employed over 300 people, and he spared no expense when it came to having the best-looking and best-performing manufacturing facility. There was even a wellness center on-site. He had put together flexible work hours, tons of great perks, and what he considered to be a "fun" work environment. He would hire the best consultants and trainers to come in and help his sales team and factory workers perform better and improve productivity.

Despite these perks, Harry ruled with an iron fist around the office. He was focused, driven, and highly controlling. Nobody messed with Harry. He was all business all the time. He had built a culture around words like "performance," "excellence," and "work ethic." He believed that if everyone just worked as hard as he did, they could have anything in life they wanted. As far as Harry was concerned, he was a top-shelf employer—offering good wages, excellent benefits, and a stable work environment. What more could people ask for?

But there was a problem. Harry's employees just didn't seem to appreciate all the wonderful things Harry had done for them. As far as Harry was concerned, every time he would do something nice for them, they'd come back up asking for (or demanding) more.

What really put Harry over the edge was when he went to conduct a site visit for his flour supplier. The supplier was a small business with around 30 employees. Their facility was nothing like the gorgeous, cutting-edge facility that Harry's was. There was no wellness center, flex hours, or cash bonus program. Yet the employees at his vendor's facility seemed to be having the time of their lives at work. They appeared to be having fun together. When he asked the company owner about it, the company owner talked about how most of the 30 employees had been working at the company for over 10 years. A handful of them were second-generation employees.

"We don't pay them much—we can't afford to. But we treat them like family and they love working here," his vendor said. "My people know how much money we make as a business and how much money I take home. They know they can trust me to do the right thing no matter what."

His vendor might as well have been speaking a different language at this point because Harry just couldn't make heads or tails of this nutty business owner's approach. "Tell them how much money we are making? Treat them like family? This guy must be off his rocker!" Harry said to himself. "Employees are there to work and then go home. If they want special attention, they need to work harder. Go make me a million bucks and you'll have all the attention you want," Harry said to his vendor friend.

"Well, that just makes us different Harry," the vendor said. "We're just cut from two different pieces of cloth."

Even though Harry knew he would have to be crazy to implement the vendor's corporate culture at his factory, he was intrigued enough to try a couple of the vendor's best-performing corporate culture ideas. The first idea Harry was going to implement was the concept of *open office hours with the company owner.* Every Friday, at the vendor's facility, the staff was welcome to bring their sack lunch into the meeting room and have lunch with the company owner. At the luncheon, no topic was off-limits. They would discuss anything from politics to home cooking and employee complaints to customer feedback. Harry's vendor was convinced this was one of the keys to the happy employees in his company.

Harry could hardly wait to get back to the office to share the good news with his team. The V12 engine of his S600 AMG roared down the M1 motorway as he made his way back to the factory. He walked into his office and summoned his no. 1 and no. 2 executives for a very important meeting.

"We're going to do things differently from now on." Harry said. "Sarah, I want you to look into catering lunch every Friday for 50 people and announce a brand-new program called *Lunch with the Boss*. Everyone is invited to come. Bring your ideas, suggestions, and even your grievances, and the boss man is ready to hear you and take action."

How do you think Harry's luncheon bonanza worked out? You probably guessed right. It didn't go too well. There were three people at the first luncheon (two of whom were the no. 1 and no. 2 execs). By week 3, Harry called the program a failure and walked away grumbling about his ungrateful employees.

Freeze Frame

As we dive deeper into Entrepreneurial DNA, it won't take you long to understand why a Friday luncheon was so successful at one company and not at Harry's. If one size fits all, then Harry's luncheon should have been just as good if not better than his vendor's. After all, Harry catered the darn event—and my guess is, the food was excellent.

So then maybe, just maybe—one size doesn't fit all.

Push Play

To Harry, the whole situation didn't make any sense.

Here's what else didn't make sense to Harry. He couldn't understand why the average employee tenure at his vendor's company was over 10 years. Meanwhile, the average executive in his organization lasted less than 18 months. As Harry surveyed his human resources (HR) story with me, all I could picture was a two-way door to his executive suite. One day you're in and the next day you're out. Some of his most talented people were now with competitor companies or running their own companies.

"Why did they have to leave?" he questioned. "I had given them the opportunity of a lifetime here. I gave them a better opportunity than any of my competitors and certainly a better income opportunity than my crazy vendors down south. I don't get it."

Harry in his own way—just like James, Alex, and Gina—had fallen victim to the unspoken rules of old school entrepreneurship. He felt like a loser when he compared himself to someone he considered a peer—another business owner.

So What Now?

Hopefully as you read through some of these real-life stories, you found yourself and some of your business frustrations in them. The fact is, I could tell 50 more stories just like them. Stories of entrepreneurs, like you and me, struggling to find a firm footing to stand on and build actionable strategy on.

- If people like Harry keep deploying HR strategies that they borrow from their vendors, people like Harry will continue to be disappointed.
- If couples like Alex and Gina continue to dump their life savings, blood, sweat, and tears into businesses that look good on the surface but have no chance of succeeding under their watch, entrepreneurship will continue to get a bad rap.
- If guys like James keep buying into the sick game that many information marketers and business opportunity promoters keep pitching—"Person X made a million bucks doing this and so can you," there will continue to be a lot of pain in the marketplace.

Now here's the really crazy part. If we had these four individuals switch places in each other's companies, there is a pretty good chance they could have had a more successful outcome. Alex and Gina aren't doomed from the world of business. They may have had great success running the company James was running. They just weren't built to handle the company they happened to purchase. Indeed, after discovering their individual Entrepreneurial DNAs, the entrepreneurs were able to make adjustments to their businesses and are now experiencing more success and are happier with their businesses

Here's my point. All entrepreneurs have an equal opportunity to succeed in the marketplace *if* they take into account their Entrepreneurial DNA when selecting, starting up, growing, and selling their ventures.

Put another way, here is the thesis of this book: *Best business results come after you have mastered your Entrepreneurial DNA and optimized your business plan for your unique gifts, strengths, and weaknesses.*

Now it is time for you to discover your Entrepreneurial DNA so you can go on to build and deploy a strategic business plan that is perfectly suited for who you are.

4

Discovering Your BOSI Profile

BOSI (pronounced "bossy") is the acronym for the four Entrepreneurial DNAs—the Builder, the Opportunist, the Specialist, and the Innovator. In a moment, you are going to have a chance to discover which of these Entrepreneurial DNAs are present in you and drive your business decisions. This will be your BOSI profile. But first, here are a few ground rules.

Time to Power Down the Engines

I am amazed at people who can read through a book in a day or even in a single sitting. It takes me weeks! If you happen to be a gifted speed-reader (or suffer from mild-to-advanced attention deficit disorder), I want to ask you to power down your engines for the next five to eight minutes. You are about to take a short assessment that will help you discover your BOSI Profile. The assessment is essentially five statements made by each of the four Entrepreneurial DNA types. Your goal is to pick the statement that fits you the *most* in *each* of the five cases.

If you hurry through the process, you'll probably misdiagnose yourself. A statement made by one of the Entrepreneurial DNA types may sound just close enough that you may select it without really pondering the other options. Please take the time to read each statement carefully and come back to select the one that *best* fits you at this time.

Make Authenticity Your No. 1 Objective

I remember taking my first Myers–Briggs Personality Test. I had applied for an internship with a Fortune 100 insurance company. I was so excited about the possibilities of having that brand on my college résumé that I was willing to do almost anything to get the internship. I was even willing to "help" myself look as good as possible on the test results. So I proceeded to answer questions based on the principle of "I know what I *would* say, but what *should* I say?" If you have ever taken a Myers–Briggs test, you know I was dreaming to think that I could "outdo" the sophistication of the test.

As it relates to the assessment you are about to take, it contains only ten questions (not a complex web of a hundred questions designed to keep you from tricking the system). I value your time as an entrepreneur and know that you're not going to sit there for 45 minutes taking a complex assessment. So this one will take you less than five minutes.

You have to resolve to be *absolutely authentic* in your choices. Here's why. If you attempt to do what I did with my first Myers–Briggs test, you will end up with an incorrect BOSI Profile. Everything I have to share with you in the pages to come—from simple tips to advanced business strategy—feed from this BOSI Profile. With an incorrect BOSI Profile, you could end up building and deploying a strategy that is harmful to your business. Be authentic, and you'll see some remarkable results.

Taking the BOSI Assessment

Point the Web browser of your computer or smart phone to www.bosidna.com/test. It will take you less than 5 minutes to complete the test and generate your *unique* BOSI Profile. So take 5 minutes to go online right now so you can continue your journey through the book.

If you don't have access to the Internet right now, you can take the mini-test below so that you can generate a quick BOSI Profile and continue with the book. However, make sure to take the free online test at your earliest convenience. It will give you a much more accurate picture of your Entrepreneurial DNA and also provide you with your comprehensive BOSI report.

The Quick BOSI Test

Circle the statement (A–D) in each section (1–5) that resonates MOST with you:

Section 1
A. I started my business so I could be my own boss and earn a bigger income than an employer could pay me.
B. I would be happy if everyone could have my product/service for free. I didn't go into business to make a bunch of money.
C. I am an entrepreneur because building companies is what I do and have always done. I have done it with great success.
D. I am always open to looking at ways to develop wealth by working *smarter not harder.*

Section 2
A. I have started up companies in more than one industry. Most of the businesses I have started up are still in existence today.
B. I spend a majority of my day providing the primary service/product to our customers.
C. In business, timing is everything. Being at the ground floor is a key to making big money.
D. Running and managing a business is something I am not made to do. It almost pushes me to a nervous breakdown.

Section 3

A. I am an optimist. Despite past setbacks, I am confident I am going to make it *big* on my current venture.

B. Beyond just conceptualizing a business idea, I can put together the business plan, raise the money, recruit the management team, and get the business profitable with ease.

C. My business first started because people loved my product. I would have been happy just to give it to them, but people told me I was nuts not charging for it.

D. Cold prospecting/calling is not something I am comfortable doing.

Section 4

A. I love the idea of working hard for a window of time (two to five years)—making a fortune and then never having to work again.

B. Standing out from our competition is a constant struggle for our company.

C. Building businesses from the ground up is fun and easy for me.

D. I feel somewhat intimidated around seasoned businesspeople.

Section 5

A. I'd much rather be working in the "lab" of my business than in the business office or at the cash register.

B. If someone brings me a stock tip or ground-floor income opportunity, I am likely to say yes a majority of the time.

C. I have more than 20 full-time employees working for me.

D. I am not easily distracted by other business opportunities or money-making deals.

Section	Choice (A, B, C, D)
1	
2	
3	
4	
5	

Now on the chart below, circle the *B, O, S* or *I* that matches your response for each question. For example, in Question 1, if your choice was "C", then circle the *B* in cell 1-C.

SECTION	A	B	C	D
1	S	I	B	O
2	B	S	O	I
3	O	B	I	S
4	O	S	B	I
5	I	O	B	S

You are almost done!

Now simply total up the number of *B, O, S,* and *I* responses you had and put them on this grid.

B	O	S	I

Now take the **two letters that earned the highest scores** and jot them down below. These are your *temporary* **Primary and Secondary Entrepreneurial DNAs**. I would still like you to take the full test online to ensure an accurate profile, but these results should suffice for now.

PRIMARY (highest score)	SECONDARY (next highest score)

Alert: Do not proceed through the rest of this book until you have completed your BOSI Test. Reading any further without having taken the test could skew your test results in the future.

Before we jump into a study of your Primary Entrepreneurial DNA, let's get a high-level understanding of what BOSI DNA really is. I'll explain more about what each of these letters means over the coming chapters, but for now, I'll give a brief overview.

The BOSI Quadrant

Now that you have discovered your Primary and Secondary Entrepreneurial DNAs, I want you to see the bigger picture of the BOSI Quadrant and how you fit into it. First, take a look at your profile and find where your Primary DNA falls on the quadrant following (Figure 4-1).

Figure 4-1   Your Profile

Now, let's start with a quick overview of the four DNAs.

- **The Builder DNA:** Picture Donald Trump in the boardroom scene of the TV hit *The Apprentice.* That is classic Builder DNA in action—driven, focused, cold, ruthless, and calculating. Builder DNA is the ultimate chess player in the game of business, always looking to be two or three moves ahead of the competition. This DNA loves building a business from the ground up.

- **The Opportunist DNA:** The Opportunist is the speculative part of the entrepreneur in all of us. It's the part of our Entrepreneurial DNA that wants to be at the right place at the right time, leveraging timing to make as much money as *fast* as possible. If you have ever felt enticed to jump into a quick money-making deal, a real estate quick-flip, or an initial public offering (IPO), then your Opportunist DNA was in play.

- **The Specialist DNA:** An entrepreneur with a Primary Specialist DNA will enter one industry and stick with it for 15 to 30 years. Picture the hometown dentist, the pizza shop owner, the graphic designer, the information technology (IT) expert, or the independent accountant or attorney. They build strong expertise, but struggle to stand out in a crowded marketplace of competitors.

- **The Innovator DNA:** Innovator DNA tends to manifest itself in entrepreneurs who have accidentally stumbled across a breakthrough invention, recipe, concept, system, or product that can be built into a business. This type of DNA instantly drives the entrepreneur into the "lab" of the business and gets him or her passionate about research and development (R&D). If you run into a scientist, inventor, or thought leader, chances are you'll see Innovator DNA at work.

With these four pictures in mind, let's take a quick walk around the BOSI Quadrant. I want to show you some interesting insights into the four DNAs as they share space with each other.

The Upper Quadrants (Builder and Opportunist)

Figure 4-2 Builder and Opportunist Profiles

It is interesting to note that despite their differences, the Builder and the Opportunist DNAs do have some things in common. That's why they fall *together* in the top quadrants. Entrepreneurs who have a Builder-Opportunist or an Opportunist-Builder BOSI Profiles are called "upper-quadrant" entrepreneurs. These entrepreneurs tend to have multi-industry experience. They just go about their business careers very differently. The Builder starts, builds, and sells a company. Then the Builder tends to move on to do it again and again—quite often in a totally different industry. The Opportunist, on the other hand, tends to leverage multiple business ventures at the same time with the intent of creating multiple streams of income. At the end of the day, both the Builder and the Opportunist end up having generated income from more than one industry. That's something they both have in common.

Builders and Opportunists share some other traits as well. They both tend to be big-vision, big-picture thinkers. They don't get too excited about being part of a venture that generates a few hundred thousand dollars of revenue in a year. Their juices start to flow when there is talk of being part of multimillion- or multibillion-dollar enterprises.

Upper-quadrant entrepreneurs are also bigger risk takers than their lower-quadrant counterparts. If you've ever seen an entrepreneur light his or her hair on fire and jump off a cliff (figuratively speaking, of course), I can assure you that his or her top-quadrant DNA was in high gear.

Upper-quadrant entrepreneurs share a common weakness—people—but for different reasons. For the Builder, it is hard to maintain long-term interpersonal relationships because the Builder tends to try to control people. The Opportunist tends to look at people as glorified checkbooks—a source of money, referrals, and more business. In both cases, when left unattended, the Builder and the Opportunist DNAs leave a trail of relational casualties in their wake.

When a Builder and an Opportunist get together, it is an interesting interaction to observe. The Builder takes an instant liking to the positive, energetic Opportunist. The Builder doesn't waste time trying to recruit the Opportunist to become a promoter or salesperson for the Builder's enterprise. The Opportunist, on the other hand, sees the Builder as a perfectly qualified customer for the product or service the Opportunist is already selling. If you think back to the story of Bob and Omar in the hotel lobby, you'll see Builder and Opportunist DNA in action together.

It makes for some great people-watching to see these two DNAs interact with each other and attempt to get into each other's pocketbook. In most cases, the Builder buys whatever the Opportunist is selling just to get him or her to shut up and consider the career change of coming to work with, and for, the Builder.

If you want to picture a famous top-quadrant entrepreneur in your mind's eye, picture Sir Richard Branson. His book *Screw It, Let's Do It* telegraphs his Opportunist DNA. His track record for having built highly scalable companies across several industries shows his Builder DNA.

Sir Richard Branson's healthy blend of Opportunist and Builder DNAs is what makes him successful in the marketplace. He has the blue-sky, anything-is-possible, failure-is-part-of-success mind-set of the Opportunist DNA combined with the system-designing, brand-building, global-infrastructure-creating of the Builder DNA.

The Lower Quadrants (Specialist and Innovator)

Figure 4-3 Specialist and Innovator Profiles

Specialist and Innovator DNAs (Figure 4-3) also have some things in common. As "opposites" of their upper-quadrant counterparts, they tend to be *single-industry* focused—but for different reasons. Innovators end up staying in one industry for the long haul because the research and development (R&D) engine inside them keeps developing *new products* within that industry. Specialists end up staying in the same industry because their expertise or credentials allow them to generate a *life-long revenue* stream from it.

Compared to the upper-quadrant duo (Builder and Opportunist), Specialist and Innovator DNAs are quite risk-averse. When faced with a risky start-up, expansion opportunity, joint venture, or marketing spend, they typically opt for the option with the least exposure.

Lower-quadrant entrepreneurs tend to be the small business owners around the world. They are a vital part of the entrepreneurship ecosystem because without them, the large Builder DNA companies could not exist. The Innovator's designs and the Specialist's products and services are what allow the Builder DNA companies to scale up, outsource, and thrive in the global marketplace.

The lower-quadrant duo (Specialist and Innovator) find it easier to balance work and life. They tend to maintain a fairly regular work schedule. They also have hobbies and pastimes that allow them to be distracted from the daily grind of the businesses they run. Meanwhile the upper-quadrant players can easily go completely out-of-balance and work way too many hours, with little regard for collateral damage caused to their person and loved ones.

Lower-quadrant entrepreneurs share a common weakness—business development. They look at entrepreneurs with strong Builder or Opportunist DNA and think, "Oh, my goodness! How do these people come up with all these ideas to grow their business? It's like they have a new marketing initiative every day. They seem to have no trouble going out and selling, promoting, and generating new business." Specialists and Innovators have to work extra hard to get the same business development results as the upper-quadrant duo.

The Left Quadrants (Builder and Specialist)

Figure 4-4 Builder and Specialist Profiles

Despite their many differences, the Builder and Specialist DNAs have some things in common (Figure 4-4). Both of these DNA types tend to be very methodical and systematic in their approaches to business. They are long-term planners. They find it well within their gifting to hire and manage staff. Having the corner office in a suite or a building full of employees is a vivid part of the movie playing in a left-quadrant entrepreneur's mind from the day he or she starts an enterprise.

Left-quadrant entrepreneurs can easily be perceived as cold, overconfident taskmasters. Their focus tends to be on systems and processes, so they are drawn to staff who have a strong affinity for executing the directives given to them.

Left-quadrant entrepreneurs are excellent at delegating and managing process. When you walk the halls of a left-quadrant company, you can safely expect to see lots of employees, organized meetings, standard operating procedures, and redundant systems.

Builders and Specialists also share a common weakness. They tend to be prideful, self-reliant people. They try and *do it all* and it is very hard for them to admit that they don't *know it all*. Their business experience (Builder DNA) or marketplace expertise (Specialist DNA) gives them this iconic confidence. In some cases, this confidence serves them well in a highly competitive marketplace. However, if left unchecked, this confidence can easily lead to excessive pride, ego, and self-worship. Individuals who do get to this point have the chance to end up leading cold and lonely lives with few deep and meaningful relationships.

The Right Quadrants (Opportunist and Innovator)

Figure 4-5   Opportunist and Innovator Profiles

The polar opposite of the left-quadrant duo (Builder and Specialist) is the right-quadrant duo, the Opportunist and the Innovator (Figure 4-5). This DNA pair tends to be highly creative and out-of-the box thinkers, but for different reasons. Driving the Opportunist's out-of-the-box thinking is the desire to reach his or her goal of financial freedom as quickly and efficiently as possible. This allows the Opportunist to catch and pursue leads and businesses that other BOSI DNAs could care less about. Driving the Innovator's out-of-the-box thinking is the desire to change the world and make it a better place. It allows the Innovator to sit for seemingly countless hours tinkering with his or her formula, recipe, or system. This ability for critical thinking allows the Innovator to find a way to solve a given problem.

Right-quadrant entrepreneurs are responsible for great changes in our world. The Innovators make great discoveries and the Opportunists tend to bring those great discoveries to market as salespeople and sales promoters. Unlike their left-quadrant counterparts, they love spending time with and around people. "The more the merrier" is the approach of the right-quadrant types.

Opportunists and Innovators are very open to asking for help and guidance. This willingness to ask for help allows them to counteract weaknesses of their DNA.

Right-quadrant entrepreneurs can be quite disorganized when it comes to their day-to-day lives. They procrastinate on things that they don't like to do. When you walk the halls of a right-quadrants company, you can expect to find heaps of unfiled paperwork, products that have yet to be inventoried, bills that have not been paid, and sticky notes all over their computer screens. That's because right-quadrant entrepreneurs feel they have better things to do with their time and talent than sit around creating spreadsheets and organizing systems. Truth be told, they just aren't built to do those types of structured things. Unlike their left-quadrant counterparts, who appear stoic and business-like in all their affairs, the right-quadrant duo tries to keep life and business fun, positive, and family-friendly.

Cross Quadrant DNAs (Specialist-Opportunist and Builder-Innovator)

See Figures 4-6 and 4-7 below.

Figures 4-6 and 4-7   Builder-Innovator and Specialist-Opportunist

Cross-quadrant DNA relationships end up exposing a yin-yang relationship. Specialists and Opportunists have virtually nothing in common with each other. The Specialist is methodical, calculated, and risk-averse. Meanwhile, the Opportunist is impulsive, disorganized, and risk-friendly. It is hard for this duo to get along in marketplace situations because they constantly butt heads on strategy and decision making. The really interesting scenario to study is when Specialist and Opportunist DNA manifests itself in the same entrepreneur. We'll talk more about that tug-of-war in later chapters.

Builders and Innovators are opposites as well. The Builder is the system-designing, infrastructure-loving, business-scaling machine. The Innovator, on the other hand, is the quiet, introspective, inventive genius who wants little to do with business operations.

Table 4-1 is a high-level profile summary for your reference as you read the rest of the book.

Table 4-1 High-Level Profile Summary

DNA Type	Overview
Upper Quadrant (B/O/BO/OB)	This group tends to have multi-industry experience. This gives them a bigger perspective in business planning and growth strategy. This group tends to lean toward promotional activities and business development.
Lower Quadrant (S/I/SI/IS)	This group tends to focus on one industry for most or all of their career. This allows them to build expert status in a trade. This group tends to lean toward being a service provider.
Left Quadrant (B/S/BS/SB)	This group is methodical and systems driven, prideful, and egotistical. This group is equipped to hire and manage employees, and manage infrastructure.
Right Quadrant (O/I/OI/IO)	This group is creative and impulsive. This group lacks organization and focus. This group is more comfortable without employee and infrastructure management.
Cross Quadrant (BI/IB/SO/OS)	These pairs tend to be polar opposites of each other, with almost nothing in common. Within these differences comes an opportunity to partner with their cross-quadrant peers and leverage their strengths to offset their weaknesses.

How Your BOSI Profile Works

Now that you know where you fit within the BOSI Quadrant, let's take a deeper look at how these DNA types manifest themselves as you make decisions about and run your business.

Have you ever watched the following TV commercial? The guy sleepwalks in the middle of the night down to his kitchen, over to the refrigerator, and opens it up for a midnight snack. No sooner does he open the refrigerator door than presto! An angel and a devil appear on either shoulder. The beautiful angel reminds the big guy about his last doctor's visit and his promise to his wife to eat healthy. The devil on the other side, tells the angel to go take a hike.

In that very moment, our guy is faced with a dilemma. He has to choose between two very compelling arguments. Inevitably, he makes a choice and reaps the rewards (or peril) of that decision.

Now, I want you to keep that visual in your mind as we talk about your BOSI DNA. Because your BOSI DNA pops up very much like that angel and devil do whenever a decision is being made. Now, I'll say that again, your BOSI DNA pops up *whenever a decision is being made.*

So, your BOSI DNA is involved whenever you are sitting there thinking:

- Should I hire this candidate sitting in front of me or should I not?
- Are we going to take that advertising space or not?
- Am I going to put my family first and leave the office right now or am I going to stay and work another hour or two?

Your BOSI DNA is birthed from several sources. A few of the obvious ones include your core belief systems, the environment in which you were raised, your life journey, and the influential people in your life. I am not a psychologist by trade so I'll spare you the scientific mumbo jumbo and suggest this simple thought: *Your BOSI DNA is a reflection of who you are.* Since you are not a clone of every other human being on earth, there are things that make you different. However, there are some trends we humans have in common. Personality studies have proven that over the ages.

Entrepreneurship is no different. Within the diverse world we live in, there are trends that make us very similar to certain entrepreneurs—and diametrically opposed to others. Now that you know your BOSI Profile, have a few peers take the assessment themselves and compare your profile to theirs. You'll be quite pleased to see that many of the intuitive "hunches" you had about your similarities and differences are confirmed by the profiles.

For 95 percent of us, we have all four BOSI DNAs inside us. One of those DNAs is typically dominant—your Primary DNA—while the other DNAs tend to pop up like the angel and devil every time you are making a decision. In some rare cases (5 percent of the time), you will run into entrepreneurs who are "purebreds"—scoring 10 out of 10 for just one BOSI DNA.

Fluidity—An Interesting Nuance of Your BOSI Profile

I think you get the message that your BOSI Profile is who you are as an entrepreneur. It's the engine that drives your modus operandi *today*. So, it should come as no surprise to you that your BOSI Profile changes as you change. Younger entrepreneurs can see significant shifts in their BOSI Profile as they figure out who they are in the real world and form their long-term business identity.

Here's a real-life example—my life. I've been building companies since I was age 23. If the BOSI Assessment Test had existed back then, I would have been profiled as a Primary Opportunist DNA. I wanted to get rich fast, I wanted to drive a 911 convertible, live in a brand-new custom-built home, and travel the world in style. But I didn't want to work my whole life to get there. I wanted it all before my thirtieth birthday! Naturally, I gravitated to opportunities that promised that type of a quick result.

Fast-forward a few years, and by age 27 I was involved in the start-up of a handful of companies at the same time. One company was an information technology (IT) venture. Another was a call center selling high-ticket travel. Then there was the sales training company and finally a lead generation company. In each case, I wrote the business plans, raised the money, hired the people, put the systems in place, and had the companies up and running.

That experience, concentrated over a four- or five-year window of time, caused me to begin to manifest a lot of Builder tendencies. As I was growing as a person and as an entrepreneur, my BOSI Profile was changing. As a result, my BOSI Profile changed to Builder-Opportunist. By age 35, my Primary DNA was Builder and I had a small Secondary Opportunist DNA that would sneak up on me every once in a while.

When I discovered the BOSI Quadrant, I got so passionate about what it meant for the world of entrepreneurship, that my that my Innovator DNA kicked into high gear. My current BOSI Profile is Builder-Innovator-Opportunist (BIO).

Here's the point I want to make. Let's say the BOSI Profile was never discovered. I would have no way to explain why my modus operandi and decision-making processes had changed so dramatically over the first ten to fifteen years of my business career. I had gone from a "get-rich-quick guy" to a "start-up guru" to a "mad scientist"—each with his own distinct modus operandi.

As you look back on your entrepreneurial career, you may find a similar journey. However, you may also find a very steady BOSI Profile all along the way. Just know that a change in your BOSI Profile is not a bad thing. It is only bad if you change your profile but *don't* change your strategic plan. I know too many entrepreneurs who are operating out of an outdated playbook—one that was written for them years ago, but no longer applies. That makes for a very frustrating business journey.

I'd like to recommend that if you ever sense your life journey taking a significant shift, come back and retake the BOSI Test. Check your scores and make sure the life change has not led to a different Primary BOSI DNA manifesting itself within you. If you do see your scores shift to a point where you have a new Primary DNA, make sure to come back and study the matching section of the book and make the necessary changes to your business strategy. Otherwise you stand to face a world of hurt and frustration.

So in summary, I believe that to some extent, most of us have *multiple* BOSI DNAs in us. I also believe that we have one Primary DNA that drives us at any given time. For that reason, our no. 1 objective is to look at the Primary DNA that is currently manifesting itself within you and optimize your business plan around that DNA. That's what we'll do in Part Two.

part two

How Can I Make My Entrepreneurial DNA Work for Me?

It is now time to dive into your Primary BOSI DNA. You can use the legend below to skip to the section of the book that matches your Primary DNA and learn what will work best for you and your business, or you can read straight through and gain a full understanding of all the BOSI DNA types. Over the next eight chapters, I'll illustrate how your specific BOSI DNA manifests itself at work and at home, when it's at its best and its worst, and specific strategies to implement within your business to take advantage of your DNA's strengths and mitigate its weaknesses.

- **B—The Builder DNA:** Chapters 5 and 6, Pages 51–90
- **O—The Opportunist DNA:** Chapters 7 and 8, Pages 91–129
- **S—The Specialist DNA:** Chapters 9 and 10, Pages 131–164
- **I—The Innovator DNA:** Pages 165–188

As we move through Part Two, we're going to go back to the original cast of characters from the hotel lobby bar—**B**ob the Builder, **O**mar the Opportunist, **S**ue the Specialist, and **I**ngrid the Innovator. Depending on your Primary DNA, you'll learn a whole lot more about one of these individuals, and by extension, yourself. By reading about their business successes and failures, you will gain some insight into how you can better run your business. All four of these stories are based on real-life entrepreneurs I have worked with. Their names and certain details about their companies have been changed to protect the innocent.

chapter

5

The Builder DNA: "People Drive Me Nuts"

As we saw in Part One, Builder DNA is the part of an entrepreneur's makeup that drives him or her to build highly scalable businesses and sell them for a huge multiple. In order to see how you, as a builder, should structure and manage your business, let's return to our story from Chapter 1.

Overview

Bob Morris owns a growing pizza franchise chain called Pizza Pete's, which employees 80 people in its corporate office and production facility outside of Atlanta, Georgia. Bob's mission is to build the company into a national giant before selling it to a franchise aggregator. Prior to starting this company, Bob built and sold a vending machine company and a take-out restaurant. Bob is a great example of how Builder DNA manifests itself in a business owner's actions and personality. As a Builder, these should sound familiar to you.

Built to Build

Bob feels like he was born to build businesses. From the conception of the venture, to starting, funding, growing, and eventually selling it... it's what he does and he does it well. His track record in business has been mostly wins. Very few people have a perfect record, of course, but his successes greatly outnumber his failures.

Bob has figured out and applied the "golden threads of business" successfully within his company to build it past the coveted $5 million revenue mark. Now, his company does in excess of $40 million a year in sales.

Much of Bob's joy comes from starting up and building systems. He likes creating from the ground up. Bob didn't need any educational products or "how-to" books; he did well just by instinct.

Bob doesn't allow his rules to be broken, but he is somewhat willing to break other people's rules if they get in his way. He generally doesn't want anyone telling him how to do anything. He prefers to be the one telling other people how to do things.

Even though Bob is already doing well financially, he keeps building his business. For him, it's not about personal income, its more about the size of his enterprise (square footage, number of employees, number of franchisees, annual revenues, and market dominance). That is how Bob measures himself. He won't be satisfied until he has one of the biggest and most-recognized brands in this market.

Bob finds it easy to get "in the zone" with business building. The drawback is that he finds it hard to switch "off" and relax. Although his new wife tries to get him to go on vacation, she has yet to succeed.

Bob has a high-risk tolerance. His ability to engage in risk is something he is proud of. Meet him at any party or sit next to him on an airplane and he'll have plenty of war stories about how he took that big risk when no one else was willing to. He wears it like a badge of honor.

Having employees suits Bob's style more than outsourcing and engaging independent contractors. He won't admit it openly, but he likes the control he has over his employees. Being the boss has its privileges.

Most of his employees drive Bob nuts though. They seem to come to him with the silliest questions. It's almost like when they get around Bob, they have to say something really, really foolish and emotional.

"What does Maggie's sick uncle have to do with her showing up for work on time and doing her job?" Bob thinks to himself, "Why should those two events even be connected?"

Bombs Away! The Alter Ego

Watch this movie in your mind: Bob is sitting there in his office, working away, but there is a nagging thought in the corner of his mind that something, somewhere, is amiss. It gnaws at him, and he finally starts looking over all the areas of his business. "Finance? No. Operations? No, that looks okay too. Sales? Dang it! I knew it. The sales team didn't finish the project I assigned to them two weeks ago!"

Dr. Jekyll suddenly becomes Mr. Hyde. Jumping out of his chair and storming down the hall, Bob goes from being the friendly leader to the tyrant! The employees see him coming and are reading his body language. They scatter. He corners the VP of sales and barks some orders that sound like "Sales team—conference room—now!"

Bob then proceeds to ask them some very pointed and harsh questions. The whole team seems to come apart at the seams like a cheap suit. There are a few clenched jaws and a couple of misty eyes around the conference room. The team wants to fight back and state their case, but they know better than to speak up at a time like this.

Welcome to Bob's alter ego. Bob doesn't even realize how overbearing he is. To him, he's just taking care of business. But to the folks around the table, it is an avalanche of belittlement and condescension.

This Mr. Hyde part of Bob is very temporary. As soon as the bombing run is complete, he's fine again. He goes back to being the normal, fun, entertaining, generous, and engaging personality. Fifteen minutes after the attack, he wanders out to see who wants to go to lunch at his favorite restaurant—on him. He's puzzled because no one is jumping at the chance to hang with the boss man as they usually do.

"Feed in My Pasture, It's the Greenest Here!"

Have you ever watched an episode of *Lion Kingdom* on the Discovery Channel? Picture in your mind the lion, sitting in the African Sahara under a shady tree after eating a bellyful of zebra. The lionesses and the cubs are about 40 yards away, relaxing and playing. Picture the look on that lion's face, a look of complete contentment. He lets out a huge yawn, stretches, looks over his kingdom of happy subjects, and settles down for a nap.

That's Bob in a nutshell. He gets a lot of satisfaction from looking out over his business kingdom, and seeing his happy pride. People whose mouths he's feeding, because he gave them the opportunity to work for him. In fact, it's hard for Bob to understand why anyone wouldn't want to be a part of his team forever.

Further, Bob thinks of himself as a protector and a provider. He has a hard time trying to fathom how anyone could survive in the business world without him. He tends to view his staff as sheep who will wander off, fall in a canyon, and get devoured by wild beasts without his leadership.

But the fact of the matter is that good employees do leave. People want to spread their wings, and see what else is out there. When this happens, Bob feel insulted. It is like he didn't do enough for them, so they had to go and be a part of someone else's pride. It is very hard for Bob not to take defections like this very personally.

To make sure that doesn't happen too often, Bob put together a generous compensation package and some nice perks as a way of keeping his good employees; employee ownership, flexible work schedules, stock options, on-site gym, day care, free staff meals, and a few other traditional perks are available to all card-carrying members of Bob's kingdom. Bob assumes that these perks more than make up for the extra hours and demanding workload he puts on his staff. After all, where else could they get an opportunity like the one he has given them?

Reel Them In

Bob is always recruiting. He's a salesperson at heart, because he has sales in his blood. He is either recruiting employees to work for him, bankers to put up the capital for his expansion projects, or customers to place multimillion-dollar product orders.

Bob is one of the few who actually likes staff meetings, because it's another opportunity for him to look out over his kingdom and resell his employees on the benefits of staying with him. The same rationale applies to company picnics, special dinners, or events.

And why not? After all the junk Bob has had to deal with, after all the risks he has taken, and all the personal sacrifices he has made, he takes whatever opportunity he can find to look over his kingdom, and remind himself of why he does what he does—build great businesses.

Jedi Mind Tricks

If you have ever seen a *Star Wars* movie, you know that a Jedi, a member of the Jedi Order, has a special power. When a Jedi wants to influence a decision, he simply waves his hand in front of his adversary's face. The next instant, the unassuming adversary does the Jedi's bidding.

Bob's DNA affords him this Jedi-like ability. He has the ability to engage people with his gift of communication.

This gift of communication comes with an interesting side effect, though. The people closest to Bob often find themselves wondering why they have done something they didn't really want to do. An employee might think, "I worked 60 hours this week! I gave up my weekend, I cancelled a trip with my kids, and looking back, I don't know why I did it! All my boss did was walk into my office, see how I was doing, and ask me how the project was going. When I said we were a little behind, my boss said a couple of things and made a couple of faces, and before I knew it, I was offering to stay the weekend and work extra hours. How did that happen?"

That's the Jedi mind trick. It's a classic Builder move. Bob has learned the art of *moving* people. This, like anything else, can be either good or bad. In some cases, it's an advantage that Bob can use to grow his business. He can use it as a way to get people to do things that they normally would not do, which Bob thinks is good for them, because it's taking that person to the next level. It's good for the business because it makes the business more competitive. It's good for Bob because it makes him a more effective leader.

Truth be told, Bob would admit that he has occasionally crossed the line and instead of using this skill to *motivate* people, he used it to *manipulate* them. The Jedi mind tricks can be fun within a good corporate environment. There are times when Bob's staff might laugh about it and joke about Bob, saying, "Here comes the boss! Let's see who's staying late *this* weekend!"

When this ability is used with the wrong motive, though, it can become an oppressive relationship. On occasion, resentment has built up between Bob and his employees. These loyal subjects begin to feel manipulated into doing things they do not want to do or do not feel good about doing. The long-term effects of this manipulative tendency have caused key employees to leave.

The Achilles' Heel

Bob battles relationship issues, both at work and at home. This is typically because he is driven, impatient, motivated, and always on the go. The challenge is that everyone around Bob *isn't like him.*

Think of Bob as a high-performance Ferrari, going 140 miles per hour. As he goes around a bend, he finds an employee going 25 miles per hour and saying, "Hey, can you slow down and help me?"

"Are you kidding me?" Bob thinks to himself.

If Bob doesn't slow down to handle this request, and the employee feels brushed off, then the employee will go back to his or her desk, head hung low, take the next sales call, and blow the deal. That's just how people are. They want to be around their leader, and feel cared for and understood.

However, it is really hard for Bob to slow down and deal with people only going 20, 50, or even 80 miles per hour. This is what creates a lot of relational issues for him.

Relationships are Bob's Achilles' heel. If Bob invests the time and leverages the tools to keep healthy relationships, he'll be a more effective CEO. However, if Bob lets nature take its course, the results could spell disaster.

I wish I could sit down with Bob and say, "Bob, you don't want to look back over your life and say, 'If I could do it all over again, I would do it differently. I wouldn't have been so harsh on my employees. I should have spent time getting to know what drives them. Too late now . . . but that's what I would have done.'"

Bob has some incredible business-building gifts, but he also has some crushing weaknesses. Imagine what could happen if he made some adjustments in his strategic plan for business and life. Imagine Bob working to *grow his gifts* instead of giving in to his weaknesses. He could build a billion-dollar company and a remarkable life!

High and Low Builder DNA

For purposes of our discussion over the next few pages, I want to introduce you to the concept of high and low Builder DNA. Put simply, if you earned a high number of points on the BOSI Assessment for Builder DNA, you are *high* Builder DNA. If you earned a relatively lower number of points, consider yourself *low* Builder DNA.

Builder DNA at Work

Work happens to be a Builder's playground. Builders are at their best in this environment. As in Bob's case, interpersonal relationships can be a challenging gauntlet for those with Builder DNA. One moment everyone loves you; another moment, everyone is grumbling about you at the water cooler.

Builders enjoy being around high-output people. As long as the topic of discussion is business development, visioning, strategic planning, and deal pipeline, those with Builder DNA have plenty to contribute. As soon as the conversation switches to operations, bookkeeping, checklists, and employee issues, Builders start to zone out. For this reason it is important to keep entrepreneurs with Builder DNA out of the nitty-gritty, day-to-day details of a business.

Builder DNA thrives in environments where systems can be built quickly and scaled up. Builders do not like to be placed in situations that are monotonous, repetitive, or unscalable.

Builder DNA at Home

Home can be a very interesting place for Builder DNA. There are really two levels at which Builder DNA operates at home. Level 1 is "work mode" and Level 2 is "relax mode." Work mode is typically most prevalent right when the entrepreneur gets home or when a work emergency is taking place after hours. During these times, Builder DNA can be quite damaging to the culture at home. An unprepared family member who does not know how to read the "work mode" signals can easily walk into a trap and find him- or herself the recipient of harsh words and unsolicited outbursts of anger.

Once in "relax mode," Builder DNA is very social, fun-loving, caring, and always looking to provide a safe and comfortable environment for family members. An entrepreneur with Builder DNA in relax mode is typically found experimenting in the kitchen, cleaning up, organizing, playing with the kids, and enjoying time with a spouse.

A family that understands Builder DNA—how to read the signs, and adapt to work mode and relax mode—tends to have a fairly healthy lifestyle. However, a majority of families don't understand Builder DNA (neither does the entrepreneur *with* the Builder DNA). As a result, many Builder DNA families end up dysfunctional; they are riddled with strife, resentment, fractured relationships, and oftentimes divorce.

Builder DNA at Its Best

Builders are at their best when there is something that needs to be built or designed from the ground up. This is why Builder DNA is almost a requirement for healthy start-up businesses. Builder

DNA tends to drive an individual to think globally and build systems and processes that are highly scalable. As a result, brands built by Builders tend to grow much faster and larger than those built by people with other BOSI DNAs.

Builders are also at their best when problems need to be solved. Problem solving at the highest levels comes quite naturally to those with this DNA. As a result, Builders thrive on it. The more complex or unsolvable the situation, the better it is for this DNA.

The thrill of *building new things* and *solving complex problems* is what Builders thrive on.

Builder DNA at Its Worst

Builders are at their worst when they cannot control a given situation or when the results of a given situation are not in line with the Builder's expectations. An employee who does not show up on time (or does not show up at all) puts a Builder in a twist. Similarly, when a Builder finds a situation where a major oversight by a staff member has led to some sort of damage, the same reaction occurs.

Builders tend to trust individuals and situations for specific outcomes and tend not to micromanage situations at first. However, when things don't go according to plan, Builders get overly aggressive, frustrated, and disappointed in the individual or about the situation. Depending on the severity of the mistake, Builders almost always switch to micromanager mode—which typically solves the problem, but leaves a wake of collateral damage.

Ideal Business Ventures for Builders

Start-ups, turnarounds, and high-growth companies are the best business environments in which to flourish for those with Builder DNA. Once a venture achieves its cyclical plateau in growth, Builders get very bored and antsy. If the venture hits another growth curve, the Builder settles into the typical routine of business building. However, if growth is flat or slow for an extended period of time, Builder DNA often causes the entrepreneur to micromanage situations and people, which leads to unfavorable consequences.

Builders tend to thrive most when the product or service of the venture has mass appeal (a large target audience) and the business model is highly scalable. A venture with a limited audience or scalability should be a red flag to an entrepreneur with Builder DNA (especially high Builder DNA).

Businesses for Builders to Avoid

Builders have a very hard time conforming to existing rules and systems. Therefore prebuilt business opportunities such as multi-level marketing (MLM), franchising, and dealerships are not a good fit for those with high Builder DNA. In cases where individuals with high Builder DNA do buy into franchises, you'll find that they are actively involved in the early stage of the venture and quickly move to expand to multiple locations. After that, they check out of the office and are typically found at a golf course or country club.

Individuals with low Builder DNA are much more open and adaptable to prebuilt business opportunities. However in contrast to other BOSI DNAs, like Specialists and Opportunists, prebuilt opportunities are by far the least favorable venture choice for Builders.

Some Tips on Partnerships and Alliances

In the course of everyday business, every entrepreneur is faced with opportunities to partner and align with other entrepreneurs. Builder DNA is typically very open to enter into partnerships and alliances. However, if those partnerships and alliances are entered into without careful consideration of the other BOSI DNAs involved, there could be significant damage in the future.

Builders (especially those with high Builder DNA) cannot survive in the same business venture with other high Builder DNA business owners. If you have heard the adage "butting heads," that is exactly what two high Builder DNA entrepreneurs will do all day long if they are placed in leadership positions at the same venture. There can only be one head chef in the kitchen and no self-respecting Builder DNA entrepreneur will want another Builder DNA calling the shots in his or her business.

In a good-better-best scenario, here are some tips on business partnership.

Good Scenario: Builder DNA Partnered with Specialist DNA

This makes for a reasonable business relationship. I am a big fan of Michael Gerber's work in his book, *E-Myth*. In the book, Mr. Gerber describes the frustrations that come when an entrepreneur finds him- or herself stuck working IN the business rather than ON it. This isn't the last time you'll see me refer to Mr. Gerber's work, but here is how it applies in the world of Entrepreneurial DNA. The Builder DNA will automatically focus on matters related to working ON the business while the Specialist DNA will gravitate to working IN the business. That's why Builder DNA partnered with Specialist DNA can be a good thing. Although there will be some butting of heads along the way, the Specialist DNA's desire for long-term interpersonal relationships will always mend any short-term damage.

Examples of Builder DNA partnered with Specialist DNA are seen quite a bit in the professional services industry. When a doctor, financial planner, certified public accountant (CPA), or lawyer has Builder DNA, they effortlessly recruit other doctors, financial planners, CPAs, or lawyers with Specialist DNA to join their firm as a "partner." For all intents and purposes, the Specialist DNA entrepreneurs work for the Builder DNA entrepreneur. There is an "unspoken" understanding among those partners that the managing partner has certain "gifts" that allow him or her to operate the business in a way that the other partners can focus on doing what they are really good at doing—without worrying about operational and management headaches.

Better Scenario: Builder DNA Partnered with Opportunist DNA

Builder DNA makes an entrepreneur a big picture thinker. So it is reasonable to see why a Builder is drawn to an Opportunist. Opportunists love being around big picture thinkers. Think back to the story at the beginning of this book when Omar met Bob for the first time in the hotel lobby bar. Omar was so excited to be around a successful guy like Bob because Bob was Omar's ticket to riches. Opportunists look at a business as a vehicle. So if an entrepreneur with Opportunist DNA is involved in a business that is the equivalent of a Toyota, he or she will gladly vacate that business to jump into a business that is the equivalent of a Ferrari.

Builders tend to build the Ferrari-like businesses that Opportunists can leverage to get to their goals faster. This is why at the head of every franchise brand, agency, or MLM company, you will find an individual with Builder DNA who conceptualized the venture and set it up for scalable expansion. From Domino's Pizza and Northwestern Mutual Life to Amway and FedEx, you'll find this to be the case.

Within the agent, dealer, franchisee, or distributor base of the Builder company, you will typically find entrepreneurs with Opportunist DNA leveraging the systems already put in place by the Builder. That is the good side of the relationship between Builder and Opportunist DNAs. Builders know how to get Opportunists to get out and generate revenues. In turn, Opportunists love the freedom to sell and promote knowing that the headaches—of business operations, brand management, financial reporting, and legal protection—have been taken care of by someone with Builder DNA.

The not-so-good side of the Builder-Opportunist relationship manifests itself when the entrepreneur with Opportunist DNA catches scent of a "bigger and better" business opportunity. It is very hard to keep an Opportunist focused on a venture for the long term. So Builder companies typically have a fast-revolving door of salespeople, agents, franchisees, or distributors. This is a necessary evil of the game we play.

Best Scenario: Builder DNA Partnered with Innovator DNA

When you look at the BOSI Quadrant, you'll see that Innovator DNA is cross-quadrant to Builder DNA. That typically means that the strengths of one DNA are the weaknesses of the other, and vice versa. This makes the Builder-Innovator team quite formidable in the marketplace.

Here's why. Innovators typically want nothing to do with designing and deploying business strategy. They are all about designing breakthrough products. A mad scientist, head chef, idea generator, inventor, or author would love nothing more than to have someone who can take their product to market for them. Nobody is better suited to do that, and do it on a mass scale, than an entrepreneur with Builder DNA. Companies like Google, Apple, and Kodak are just a few of the many examples of ventures where Innovator DNA and Builder DNA came together to create something amazing in the marketplace.

When you look at the temperament of the typical Builder and the typical Innovator, you will find a great match there as well. The Builder is usually driven, controlling, egotistical, and results-oriented. The Innovator is typically introspective, forgiving, friendly, trusting, and quality-oriented. The Innovator is more likely to handle the outbursts and demands of the Builder than others—this is in the Innovator's nature. Innovator DNA also balances the sharp edges that come with Builder DNA in interpersonal relationships. In a corporate environment, a Builder ends up forming a very effective good-guy–bad-guy team. Staff, suppliers, and clients find it very easy to identify which partner to go to given a specific agenda. "Good news always goes to the Builder and bad news is always given to the Innovator." That is the mantra of the individuals surrounding this best-case scenario team.

Other Tips on Collaboration

As a Builder, you know that Builders generally do not like management by committee. So avoid situations where you are one vote of many. It is too frustrating for Builders to see good ideas go to waste when others don't see eye-to-eye with them.

If you are getting ready to start a new enterprise and are thinking about bringing in one (or many) partners, make sure those individuals take the BOSI Test and don't show the exact

BOSI Profile as yours. Try and align with individuals who have cross-quadrant or complementary BOSI DNA to yours. That will result in healthier, long-term relationships and better chances for success. There are some great tools at the BOSI Web site that will help you evaluate potential peers and partners, and get some additional insight from us.

Some Typical Statements Made by the Purebred Builder:

If you have ever made any of these statements, you have been exhibiting Builder tendencies. Given your new knowledge about your Entrepreneurial DNA, think about these for a few minutes and see how they fit with your business.

- I am an entrepreneur because building businesses is what I do and have always done. I have done it with great success.
- I have started up companies in more than one industry. Most of the businesses I have started up are still in existence today.

> **BOSI BUSINESS STRATEGY ALERT!**
>
> Make sure you have not surrounded yourself with "yes men and women" in and around your company. Instead balance your tendency to make solo decisions with a team of advisors who have the ability to truly influence your decisions and hold you accountable.

- I find it easy to conceptualize new business ventures. Beyond the concept, I can put together the business plan, funding, management team, and operating plan fairly effortlessly.
- If you gave me a challenged business and a few hours or days to dig into it, I can "paper napkin" a solution and turn it around in no time at all.
- Building businesses from the ground up is fun and easy for me.

- I'd much rather start a company from scratch and control 100 percent of the brand message than buy into an existing business system.
- I feel like I have the "golden threads of business" ingrained in my mind now. I can walk into virtually any business and apply those principles to build a highly successful company.
- I find it very irritating when employees bring their personal issues to work. Worse yet, when they bring them directly to me.
- I have a hard time slowing down to answer silly questions or deal with emotional people.
- I can be Dr. Jekyll and Mr. Hyde within a very short period of time. One minute, I'm the fun-loving leader everyone wants to be around. The next minute, I notice something I don't like and I tear people apart with my words and body language.
- I have this weird ability to get people to work extra hours and give up weekends without even having to ask for it. It is like having the ability to do Jedi mind tricks.
- People often call me a "great salesperson."
- I am 24/7 when it comes to my business.
- I find it hard to take vacations.
- I am accused of being a "Type A" personality.
- I have a tendency to burn employees out. They end up leaving me for greener pastures.
- It is hard for me to balance my work and family life.

BOSI PERSONAL STRATEGY ALERT!

Take a detailed inventory of key relationships in your life over the past 10 years. How many are still healthy and strong? How many are damaged or fractured?

You must find a way to overcome your predisposition to control and manipulate others. Instead, work on nurturing and nourishing relationships with employees, associates, and even family.

- I can motivate people around me to do things that they would not normally do.
- I feel like the only reason people are around me is because they can get something from me (a paycheck, a business opportunity, a roof over their heads).
- I find it quite easy to raise money, sell to customers, and recruit employees into my business.
- I am a systems-driven business person. I like setting up systems for my staff to follow.
- My sales and marketing teams frustrate me because they don't grow the business as fast as I have planned it to grow.
- I wish people would have more of an ownership mind-set in this business. They could achieve so much more if they just gave this business their true focus and passion.
- It is lonely at the top. I find it hard to find close business and life connections.

The Builder DNA at a Glance

STRENGTHS	WEAKNESSES	FRUSTRATIONS
Builders apply the "golden threads of business" to build systems and highly scalable, sellable ventures.	Work/life balance is generally out of balance for an extended period of time, leading to collateral damage.	Builders are frustrated by people who don't perform to their extremely high expectations.
A majority of time is spent working on the business because the Builder has people and systems who work in the business.	If left unchecked, both home and business relationships become strained and fractured.	Builders are frustrated being surrounded by fair-weather fans and friends.
Builders are natural-born leaders. Potential investors, employees, and customers are drawn to their vision and brand.	Builders find it extremely hard to ask for help. They find it even harder to back down from a disagreement.	Builders are frustrated by employees who do not take total ownership of their work.

chapter

6

Seven Business Optimization Strategies for Builder DNA

The Builder DNA in you allows you to do some pretty amazing things in the marketplace. We learned about those unique strengths in the previous chapter. But we also learned about some compelling weaknesses. This chapter is designed to give you some *actionable strategy* on how to leverage your innate strengths while compensating for an optimization process. In some cases, we will be fixing something that is broken. In other cases, we will be taking proactive and precautionary strategies. In a couple of areas, we may not have to do a thing! You may have intuitively taken the necessary optimization steps already.

A business that is not optimized to your Entrepreneurial DNA is going to be very frustrating for you to be around. The seven strategies we will be discussing in this chapter are designed to make sure your playbook is designed exclusively and specifically for you. The seven strategies we'll discuss are:

- Optimize Your Business Model
- Optimize Your Organizational Structure
- Optimize Your Business Development
- Optimize Your Financing and Exit Strategy
- Optimize Your Relationships
- Optimize Your Advisory Team
- Optimize Your Personal Leadership Development Plan

I'm basing these strategies on having watched hundreds of Builders get it wrong and a handful get it right. Trust me when I say that you want to be part of the smaller group.

Strategy One: Optimize Your Business Model

You were built for highly scalable business models. You're not the person who should be buying a franchise; you are built to be the franchisor. You are a brand *builder*, not someone else's brand *expander*. You are at your best when you are building systems and companies from the ground up, so make sure you are in an environment that allows you to do that. If you happen to be working under someone else's brand, you will find your frustration levels growing by the day. You'll feel like a caged animal. Make sure you have positioned yourself in the captain's chair with the full freedom and control to design and deploy your brand into the marketplace. Start over if you have to and build something from the ground up. That's what you are made to do.

Also, make sure that your business model allows you to continue expanding into new markets. The kiss of death for your DNA is to be in a business environment that is the status quo. Your DNA requires growth. You feed on it. So look at your business plan as it exists today. Is your business model scalable to the point where you could spend the next two lifetimes doing just that? If so, you have the right business model for your company. If you find your company in auto-pilot mode with limited-to-no growth initiatives on the table, you are going to be outside your giftedness. You'll start to micromanage the business and get involved in operational areas in which you have no business being. Dust off your original business plan if you have to. Get focused on expansion and stay in the helicopter rather than fighting in the weeds.

I have found that there is a danger zone for Builder DNA that starts right around $5 million in revenues and carries through to around $25 million in revenues. If you are the CEO of a company in that revenue band, this first optimization point is critical for you. Most Builder CEOs work like crazy to get their company from zero to $5 million. They do it almost effortlessly (relative to the other BOSI DNAs). But somewhere between $5 million and $25 million, the business itself sucks the CEO into the core operations and the fun, excitement, and passion of business *building* just about evaporates. The CEO goes from race car driver to pit crew manager. If you find yourself stuck in this band with slow-to-stagnant revenues, company morale, and/or performance, it is time for you as the Builder to get re-energized. The way Builders get re-energized is by going back to the drawing board and designing the next set of big plays (including a couple of gutsy "Hail Marys"). Put another way, breakthrough ideas and strategies are what Builder DNA gets fired up and passionate about.

Strategy Two: Optimize Your Organizational Structure

Take a look at your organizational chart for a moment. How is your company structured? Is there a layer of empowered management between you and the masses? There should be.

Here's why. Remember the Dr. Jekyll and Mr. Hyde thing? You need to protect your staff from the inevitable.

Remember the Jedi mind trick part? You shouldn't always be the person making sure things get done—or you risk overusing this gifting on less-important, low-priority matters and leaving nothing in the arsenal for when you really need it.

Remember your Achilles' heel? You'll burn out relationships, especially with those who have very dominant or passive personality styles.

You are the Ferrari going 140 miles per hour and you must put systems in place to protect yourself from running into 35-mile-per-hour staff members. You should have one to five high-output leaders on your management team (depending on the size of your company) who are managing your company's operations and the day-to-day interactions within it. Figure 6-1 shows the ideal organizational structure that matches your entrepreneurial DNA:

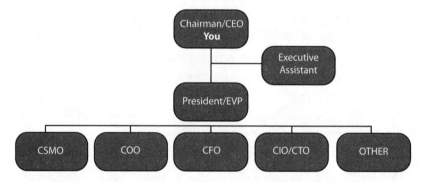

Figure 6-1 Ideal organizational structure for entrepreneurial DNA.

I'm sure your human resources (HR) expert could argue with this organization chart based on your company's specific needs. I don't want to oversimplify a very complicated area of business.

However, here are the things that are very important for your Entrepreneurial DNA:

You should not be managing the day-to-day operations. You need a president or an executive vice president (EVP) doing that for you. He or she is the most important leader in your organization. Chances are you have had your managers take a personality assessment like the Dominence, Influence, Steadiness, Conscientiousness (DISC) Profile, the Myers-Briggs Test, or the Team Dynamics CARE Profile. Each of these tests is designed to identify an employee's modus operandi and gifting (much like the BOSI Assessment Test is designed to identify yours).

The ideal DISC Personality Profile for your president or EVP will be high in DI (dominance and influence). But don't stop there. Make sure he or she has a good amount of S (steadiness) that will allow him or her to be patient and thoughtful around you. Without that, you'll butt heads with each other too often. He or she must have a level of submission in order to thrive in your organization for the long term. Skip the S (steadiness) and you'll churn through company leadership time and time again. Worse yet, you'll be training your competition's next president or EVP.

If you use the Team Dynamics CARE profile in your organization instead of DISC, your president or EVP must be high in the A (advancer) category. At the BOSI Web site, we also have some management assessment tools that will match your BOSI Profile to the gifting of your current or future managers.

Here is the bottom line. If you are frustrated with the day-to-day operations of your company, look no further than who is sitting in the chair of "day-to-day operations management." If it's you, get out of the chair. If it is someone else, have him or her assessed to ensure that he or she has the right gifting for the job (and more importantly, the right match for your BOSI Profile). If he or she doesn't show the characteristics described here, give him or her another seat on the bus (even if he or she is a beloved family member).

Make sure your chief sales and marketing officer generates a minimum of 30 percent of his or her compensation based on the company's *current* performance. Your Entrepreneurial DNA has an insatiable desire for growth. You feed on it. So make sure the most important person on your sales and marketing team isn't sitting in the lap of luxury if your company's growth rate doesn't mirror that.

Make sure that the rest of your management team— chief financial officer (CFO) or chief operating officer (COO)—are the right fit for you (based on your BOSI Profile) *and* your current stage of business. I have spent time with many CEOs whose companies have long outlived the services of the founding CFOs or COOs—yet for loyalty's sake, those individuals still have a seat at the king's table. In other situations, I have assessed management teams who are simply not fit for high-growth situations. They are better suited to run a company in "maintenance mode."

Measure the Entrepreneurial DNA of your managers and executives so that they match yours. Managers and executives have entrepreneurial gumption inside themselves as well. It is that entrepreneurial gumption that drove them to surpass their peers and become leaders in your organization. If you get the sense that your management team may need to be optimized to fit your growth-focused business model, take the necessary steps to evaluate their gifting. Then take the very important step of comparing their gifting to yours. I believe your company will be head-and-shoulders above the competition if you implement this underused human resource strategy.

Don't place family members or close friends in this top layer of management unless they have legitimately beat out other candidates for the position. Family and close friends may have been an integral part of helping your company get off the ground. But as you evaluate the next chapter of your company's story, ask yourself the candid and important question: Should these individuals remain on your management team for the go-forward? Your company will be the better for it.

Strategy Three: Optimize Your Business Development

As a Builder, you are a master of business development. As you continue to grow your business, think about business development as encompassing three main areas of your company: brand positioning, marketing, and sales.

Area 1: Brand Positioning

Brand is the ethos of your business. It defines who you are as a company and who you are *not*. It sets the culture within which your company operates, markets, services customers, and manages relationships. Most entrepreneurs think that brand is all about picking a logo, some color schemes, and business stationery. Far from it, brand is the engine that drives all marketing and sales systems. Brand sets the message of who your company is. Marketing communicates that message to your target audience in a way that gets them to respond. Sales then takes that response and converts it into new business.

If you have not taken the time to do a comprehensive brand-positioning exercise in the last 12 months, this is a mission-critical time to do so. As you master your Entrepreneurial DNA and start to make adjustments to your business plan, you must revisit your brand position. I've included my favorite brand-positioning exercise, along with detailed instructions in Exercise 3 (Chapter 13).

If you have partners or a management team, schedule an off-site retreat with them and do the exercise together. You'll be glad you did.

Area 2: Marketing

Armed with the results of a fresh brand-positioning exercise, you'll be ready to take a look at your current marketing systems to make sure you are communicating the right messages to the right audiences. It is amazing to see how many of us get caught up in the day-to-day rush of getting customers that we don't realize how many inefficiencies lie in our marketing systems. Add in the fact that over time, sales managers, marketing directors, and ad agencies come to the table with their own ideas and agendas. Before you know it, a company can get overloaded with complicated and inefficient marketing systems.

Take a walk through the "SPACE funnel" in Appendix A. At each stage of the funnel process, ask your marketing team what steps or processes and tools are currently in place to find suspects and move them from prospect to account, account to client, and client to evangelist. This will ensure you have an optimized marketing funnel.

Once you have optimized your marketing funnel, have your accountant or CFO do an analysis on the places you spend money generating leads today. Chances are you'll see a decreasing trend from traditional advertising sources like print and direct mail. It may be time to move your marketing spend to more profitable lead sources. Do the search engines consider your Web site(s) an authority? If not, you must make the investment to achieve that status. The barriers to entry for search engine authority will continue to grow and so will the costs. Now is the time to get it done so the roots of your authority can grow deep, making it almost impossible for competitors to uproot you in the future. The same is true for social media.

As you know, with Builder DNA comes a desire to control everything. Entrepreneurs with high Builder DNA tend to hire as many employees as possible for that very reason. Builder DNA loves the idea of having an in-house design, Web development, and an online marketing team.

Unfortunately, that is typically not the most optimal move in today's marketplace. The world of search engine optimization (SEO), search engine marketing (SEM), social media, and online marketing is changing at such a rapid pace, in-house employees will have a hard time keeping your company on the leading edge.

I have seen many Builder DNA entrepreneurs have greater success by outsourcing parts of their SEO, SEM, social media, and online marketing to vetted firms who eat, breathe, and sleep this stuff. Outsource marketing firms also have the ability to scale up and scale down as you need them to. They don't call in sick and they won't tell you they need time off for kindergarten graduation.

Area 3: Sales

If your brand is positioned correctly and your marketing systems are operating at their optimum level, your sales team will feel like they have been given the fun job of shooting fish in a barrel using a shotgun. CEOs with Builder DNA waste a lot of time and energy trying to figure out how to get a sales team to perform better. The truth is, in most cases, the problem is at the brand level and occasionally at the marketing level. Very seldom is the issue at the sales level. However, here are some pointers on how to make sure your sales organization is optimized for your BOSI Profile.

Roller-coaster morale within the sales organization is a common occurrence in Builder DNA companies. It goes back to your Entrepreneurial DNA and how you handle disappointment when people don't perform to your high standards. It is quite common for Builder DNA companies to develop an "us versus them" mentality between the sales team and company ownership.

Sometimes this "us versus them" mind-set is okay. It drives the sales team to work harder and reach the leadership levels of your organization. But if left unchecked, it can lead to a revolving door of talent and the resulting high costs of HR.

Given your Builder DNA, it is important for your sales team to see you as their biggest fan, not their coach. You must be perceived as the "good guy." Your sales director should be perceived as the whip-cracking sergeant or coach. Despite your greatest desire to get in the trenches, don't try to be the coach who knows every single player's strengths, weaknesses, and failures. Be the team owner who just wants the team as a whole to win the championship.

To protect your sales organization from the ill effects of the "us versus them" mentality, make sure your sales director has a training regimen for the sales team that has a healthy balance between skill and personal development. I have found that a majority of Builder DNA companies have highly skilled salespeople who are *not* growing personally.

This is why the brand-positioning exercise is so important. My guess is that having a *positive* and *upbeat* culture is part of your brand essence. If so, you must be authentic to that brand position and invest in your people. Make sure your sales organization is on a steady drip of personal development and leadership development education.

Once a year, take one week and go on the road with your sales team. Do everything they do—from making phone calls and presentations to filing reports and updating the customer relationship management (CRM) system. You must walk in the shoes of your sales organization every year to ensure that your management team has not infused an unhealthy culture or system into the sales process that conflict with *your* brand position. If I had a dollar for every "aha" moment CEOs have had when comparing *their* brand position to that of their management team, I'd be a very wealthy man.

If you have not seen an episode of the TV show *Undercover Boss*, check it out. The show nails the point I am trying to make. The CEOs who went undercover in their large corporations were quick to find areas of their companies that were operating outside their vision of the core brand position.

Business development is the engine that makes the cash register ring. Since you are equipped with Builder DNA, business development is quite near and dear to your heart. A business development engine that is running well is a joy to the heart of an entrepreneur with Builder DNA. Take the time and invest the resources to make sure this engine is performing at its best.

Strategy Four: Optimize Your Financing and Exit Strategy

Financing

With Builder DNA, you have several options when it comes to financing the start-up and growth of your company. I have seen the best success come when a combination of debt and equity financing are used. The use of 100-percent debt financing isn't the best solution, especially in this banking climate where banks are taking some fairly drastic measures to curtail their exposure on lines of credit and loans. The use of 100-percent equity financing is not a good solution either. With your Builder DNA, you have the ability to scale up in sales and revenues better than any other BOSI DNA. That means your company will have the ability to enter into and service debt fairly well. If 100 percent of your financing comes from equity and you build the size of company you are capable of building, equity may end up being the most expensive money out there.

Here's an example:

If you raise $250,000 in equity financing and give up 10 percent of your company to get it, your company is worth $2.5 million at the time prior to the financing event. If you scale the company up using those resources and sell it for $10 million, that 10-percent stake is now worth $1 million to the investor. What if you had sourced some, or all, of that funding through debt financing at an interest rate of 10 percent to 12 percent instead?

The reason I am sharing this thought with you is because I have sat at many a negotiating table at the time a company was being sold. Many entrepreneurs with Builder DNA have sat at that table, looked back on their financing strategy, and regretted not having balanced debt and equity financing better. Hopefully, that won't be the case for you.

Exit Strategy

If you are building a small business, you must operate with the end in mind. In other words, you must have a firm exit strategy in place for yourself right now. If you don't have a specific exit strategy in play already, get started on it now. Builder DNA entrepreneurs without an exit strategy start to act like caged animals and things usually don't go too well in the short term for the people around them.

Your exit strategy should have two main parts to it.

1. **Exit from company management:** This goes back to the HR strategy we've been talking about. If you find yourself still working IN your business, running meetings and talking to clients, that must change. Pronto!

   Start by building a two- to three-year strategic plan for your company. In that plan, start to remove yourself from operational and management oversight in stages. The goal must be for you to be totally out of the management part of the business.

2. **The liquidity event:** This is the fun (and lucrative) exit! The same strategic plan that facilitates your exit from company management can be extended to include your exit from the company itself. There are books written that lay out all the options for building this exit strategy so I won't write another one here. What I will suggest is that *your* Builder Entrepreneurial DNA is best suited for a handful of options.

- **Public offering:** Only consider this option if you are willing to spend a minimum of three additional years as CEO of the company. Also know that the regulatory requirements to operate a public company could take you well outside your giftedness, so pursue this option with care.

- **Acquisition:** The best time to pursue the acquisition of your company is a year or two after you have exited company management. It is the only way you can walk away from the closing table a free person. If you are in any way part of the company operations going into the negotiations for the acquisition, you will have to spend a minimum of two years transitioning the company to the new ownership and management team. Hear me when I say this—as a Builder, you are NOT built for this transition process. You will age more during a two-year acquisition transition than you ever did before. Your company will not be your company. Your staff will not be your staff. Your systems will be replaced and your brand will change. No self-respecting Builder DNA entrepreneur should be around when that happens to his or her company. So plan your exit first, and then consider the sale or acquisition of your business.

- **Employee Buyout under an Employee Stock Ownership Plan (ESOP):** You may have built a culture around your company that makes it an ideal target for your employees to buy you out. Again, the only caution I would give is that you complete your exit from management before starting an employee buyout. New owners want to bring in new ideas and fresh ways of doing things. Employees buying out the former owner are notorious for that. New ideas and fresh ways of doing things can be a good or a bad thing. But given your Entrepreneurial DNA, you'll see it as a bad thing. Relationships will sour as a result. So if an employee buyout is an option you end up considering, get out of the business first, go start another company or project, and then let your employees start the buyout.

Strategy Five: Optimize Your Relationships

The reality is that strained relationships come with the territory of Builder DNA. As you read through the previous chapter, you may have made the mental note to do some relationship management. This optimization step is designed to help you do just that.

The first instinct you may have is to put off this step and deal with it at some future time. I cannot stress to you how important it is that you override that instinct and pursue this optimization step with the same passion and commitment as you did the start-up of your company.

Entrepreneurs like you have the ability to build massive companies. As a result, you get to enjoy the spoils of those results. Unfortunately, there are too many Builder DNA entrepreneurs who have the spoils and *nobody to enjoy it with*. That happens when the Builders put off this optimization step for some time in the future. The truth is, that time in the future comes too late, or it never comes at all.

The people you care about the most are the ones who are at the greatest risk when it comes to the dark side of your Builder DNA. They are the ones who have probably had to deal with countless outbursts of anger, various controlling situations, and being on the blunt end of a belittling comment from time to time. Many of these employees have quit trying and assumed you care more about your company and business than you do about them individually. Sure, they are still around. But they are operating with a ton of scar tissue around the wounds that you have inflicted on them over time.

If what I am describing right now is not an issue in your business, consider yourself very fortunate and skip to the next optimization step. If I am hitting on a sore subject in your life, please take the time to do what I am about to suggest.

In Appendix B, you'll find the "Builder's Relationship Analyzer Quiz." You can get the online version at the BOSI Web site as well. Print out as many copies as you'd like and get ready to hand them out to people in these key categories: your spouse, your children, your key managers, a random sampling of employees, and two or three suppliers.

Now notice I said "get ready" to hand them out. You will not actually hand out the quiz. You will need to find a neutral third party who can administer the hand out, the collection, and the data analysis for you. I think you know why. If you want a bunch of sunshine blown at you, administer the process yourself. Everyone will have glowing things to say. However, if you're serious about optimizing your relationships and if you want real, honest feedback, then the respondents need to know that the information is being collected anonymously by a third party.

Here are some options for the neutral third party.

• **Option 1. Survey Monkey:** I've become a huge fan of Survey Monkey (www.SurveyMonkey.com) and I am glad to promote their service as a satisfied customer. If you are moderately Web savvy, you can take the questions from the Relationship Analyzer I have provided and build an anonymous online survey yourself within five to eight minutes. Your respondents will have the peace of mind of knowing that their privacy is totally protected (they won't have to enter any identifying information). The best part is you'll have real-time access to data plus some neat analytical tools to better understand the responses.

- **Option 2. A Paid Consultant:** Hourly consultants are a dime a dozen right now. Especially those who simply have to take the ready-made Relationship Analyzer, print out five to 10 copies, hand them out to your people, and provide a confidential pickup location. Once they've collected all the surveys, they can take two or three hours to crunch the data, and provide you with a synopsis report. You'll know what to do from there.
- **Option 3. A Random Staff Member:** At your next staff meeting, do a random drawing and have that staff member administer the collection and reporting of anonymous data to you.

Take the input and feedback as just that—feedback. Then put some measures in place to repair any existing damage. Also put systems in place that will allow you to connect with these audiences outside of regular business settings to connect, build communication, and strengthen bonds.

Strategy Six: Optimize Your Advisory Team

Let's go back to the BOSI Quadrant so you can see the "why" behind what I am about to recommend you do. Take a look at where you sit on the BOSI Quadrant. Your DNA is in the upper left.

Having an advisory team and a mastermind team full of other Builders is okay, but it certainly isn't optimal. You can gain so much more if your advisory and mastermind teams represent the diversity of the BOSI DNAs.

A good *advisory team* is made up of your attorney (who will have plenty of Specialist DNA), your accountant (again, plenty of Specialist DNA) and your business development advisor (who ideally, has some Builder DNA and some Opportunist DNA). These individuals are typically fee-based advisors who can come alongside you to help you make savvy business decisions.

Your *mastermind team* is a critical piece to your success puzzle. These individuals are not fee-based advisors, but peers who are engaging in a mutually beneficial mastermind alliance with you. A typical mastermind group will meet once a month for a half-to-full day outside the office. This is the group that will help you stay centered and accountable for the strategic plan you are building. Make sure your mastermind team has a good blend of Opportunist and Innovator DNA.

Opportunists will help you see the silver lining in every situation. They will encourage you to dream big and pursue your vision when others don't. Every Builder needs an Opportunist in his or her mastermind group. The individual with the Innovator DNA in him or her will bring the empathy, love, and balance that you tend to leave out of the business environment. Since the Opportunist is an opposite-quadrant individual, many of your strengths are his or her weaknesses, and vice versa.

If you don't have a mastermind team that you are an active and regular participant in, I'd like to encourage you to get that organized immediately. Check out CEO organizations like Vistage (www.Vistage.com), where you can plug into an existing infrastructure of groups, advisors, and global networking. If your resources allow, I would certainly recommend Vistage. I have enjoyed the benefit of that organization myself and recommend it strongly. There are also free CEO groups that organize through Meetup (www.meetup.com) and LinkedIn Groups to the BOSI Web site.

Strategy Seven: Optimize Your Personal Leadership Development Plan

You schedule staff meetings, client appointments, supplier conference calls, and shareholder meetings. Once those items are on your calendar, they get done, right?

Work-Life Balance Plan

Well, you need to develop a comprehensive work-life balance plan that schedules in time for rest, relaxation, family, and spirituality. Without it, you're wasting your time building a company. You'll be rich, but you'll be a miserable, grumpy, and lonely rich person. It is built into your DNA to be an addictive person. This addictive nature applies to people, and most of all to your work.

Left unchecked, this trait will cause your business to become the overriding focus in your life and literally control *who* you are—from your personal identity to your daily choices.

Take it from a guy who knows a lot of Builders who fit the "rich but miserable" category. Developing work-life balance is as easy as scheduling some simple activities into your daily/weekly schedule that have nothing to do with your business. Treat these new activities at the same priority level as a shareholder or client meeting. It will be very hard to do at first, but you will reap the rewards.

Wellness

Do the same with your health. Hard-book three days each week to spend time doing something to improve your health. Your DNA gets bored with any sustained routine, so make sure to change things up about every 12 weeks to make sure you don't get into a rut.

Rest

Also, start to schedule regular time away from the office. Start with working from home one day per month. Then raise that to one day per week. Take one weekend a quarter away with your spouse. Without exception, take one month a year away from your business. That may sound impossible at this moment as you read this book, but I can virtually guarantee that your business will grow faster as a result of doing so.

Continuous Personal Growth Plan

I think you know that leadership development goes far beyond adding key disciplines like work-life balance, wellness, and rest.

> "They say entrepreneurship isn't brain surgery. I say it is brain surgery. It is brain surgery you do on yourself—without the anesthesia."

You must identify and pursue a personal development program that keeps your mind fed with healthy input. Builders are notorious for stopping the personal growth process when they hit a certain level of financial success in life. The mind-set says "I've arrived, and there is very little anyone else can teach me about anything." That is a very dangerous place to be. Make sure to identify one or several leaders *you* can follow. With blogs and Twitter feeds available in abundance, find a few that can keep you fed, growing, and improving as a person.

Personally, I'd like to point you to leaders who teach humility and servant leadership as part of their core programming. That is a message you need to hear over and over again (and be held accountable for). I'd also like to recommend leaders who understand the weaknesses of your Entrepreneurial DNA and focus on equipping you to be a better, more effective leader. In most cases, they too will have Builder DNA and will have stories to tell of lessons learned through their entrepreneurial journey.

Final Words about the Seven Strategies

So there we have it—seven areas where you can dive in and optimize your entrepreneurial journal based on who you are built to be. Pay extra-close attention to Strategies Five and Six. That is where you will see the most significant return on investment (ROI) for your time, attention, and resources.

Factoring In Your Secondary DNAs

Even though your Primary DNA is that of a Builder (B), there is a strong chance some of the other three DNAs are present in your system. Unless you are a purebred Builder, you have some Secondary DNA in you. Let's take a quick look at what nuances you need to watch for. It's important to understand how to identify when and how those Secondary DNAs pop up and what to do about it when they do.

Specialist DNA

The Specialist is the analytical side of you. It's the part of you that wants to slow down the decision-making process and avoid risky choices. It's the part of you that gets stuck in the well-known trap of working *in* your business rather than working *on* it. The Specialist DNA is methodical in its approach to day-to-day operations. It will feel quite comfortable in a steady and predictable workday routine. The Specialist DNA will get agitated whenever you mix things up or change the formula of how things happen around the office. When you decide to embark on a new project, launch a new marketing initiative, or bring in a joint-venture partner, the Specialist will want to challenge those plans.

The danger of having Builder DNA *and* Specialist DNA in action at the same time is that the combination makes for a very egotistical and prideful individual. You run the risk of appearing cold (Builder DNA) and regimented (Specialist DNA) to your employees. Watch for signs that you are too aloof or overconfident. Left unchecked, this could lead to blind spots in your vision and cause damage in the marketplace.

You also run the risk of building a "not so fun" brand in the marketplace. Oh, don't get me wrong, you *want* to have your brand perceived as fun, energetic, and positive. However, your Builder and Specialist DNAs will keep that from being truly authentic.

You ask, "So how do I change that Joe?"

It's simple, really. All you have to do is tap into the Opportunist and Innovator DNAs to bring some balance to your left-quadrant leaning. If your BOSI Profile does not have any Opportunist DNA or Innovator DNA, consider filling that hole with a business partner or key manager who exemplifies those traits.

On the flip side, having both Specialist DNA and Builder DNA has some positive benefits. First of all, the Specialist DNA will keep you from going overboard, implementing every great idea you come up with during your morning shower. The Specialist DNA will force you to take a more methodical and analytical approach to vetting an idea before launching it to your insiders and outsiders as a done deal.

The Specialist DNA will also drive you to build long-term relationships. Remember, the Builder in you will be quite dismissive of people who cannot serve an immediate and self-serving purpose in your business and life. The Specialist DNA will bring some balance to that mind-set and encourage you to keep building bridges, rather than burning them.

The big thing to watch out for when you have Builder DNA and Specialist DNA is the desire to control and keep every aspect of your business operation in-house. Not that having a big infrastructure is a bad thing, but just do an honest assessment of your infrastructure and evaluate the option of outsourcing some functions to domestic or off-shore firms. Take your emotion out of the decision-making process and see what shakes out. If it appears to be a prudent decision, then give it a whirl. You may find some significant improvements in company performance while seeing some dramatic boosts to your bottom line.

Here is a summary of what the Specialist DNA in you will tend to do so that you can be aware when it is manifesting itself in your decision-making processes.

- Run away from any risky situations.
- Get stuck using traditional marketing/lead generation solutions.
- Want to stay *in* the business and control the operations—while having as many employees as possible.
- Have a long-term view for the company rather than a rushed exit strategy.
- Be very methodical and analytical about decision making.
- Get comfortable and coast when company revenues hit certain milestones.
- Get out and connect/network with other business owners rather than hide in a cave.

Opportunist DNA

Get ready to have some fun if you are a Builder with an Opportunist DNA that occasionally manifests itself. The Opportunist DNA is the part of you that wants to climb every mountain and cross every sea of opportunity, no matter how harebrained it sounds or how far off course it may be from your core business. If it has the potential to make *lots of cash*, the Opportunist in you will hit the accelerator pedal.

The Opportunist is also the optimist in you. It's the part of your modus operandi that can shake off an embarrassing situation or devastating business loss and be ready for the next venture. When the Opportunist DNA is in high gear, you will be drawn to create new stuff, hire energetic people, form promising alliances, and take massive risks. These can all be very good things for your business.

However, there is a not-so-good side to this scenario. The Opportunist DNA *enables* some of the weaknesses of the Builder DNA. For example, we now know that relational conflict comes with the Builder territory. The Opportunist DNA makes it worse because it likes to procrastinate on the "hard things" in life. So when there is a need to resolve conflict through good communication, the Opportunist in you will want to put it off—because it is hard work. The Opportunist DNA can also be overly optimistic. So when a money-making opportunity comes your way, even if it is totally out of left field, the Opportunist in you will want to jump in with both feet first, even if it means tremendous risk to your core business. Be aware of that and watch for times when the Opportunist in you is getting strong. Once you pass the tipping point and let the Opportunist win, the Builder DNA in you will lose its core effectiveness.

Also recall that the Builder and Opportunist DNAs are upper quadrant. That means your big-vision, big-picture perspective is at full throttle. There is literally nothing to hold you back from lighting your hair on fire and jumping off the cliff (so to speak) when opportunity presents itself. There is very little that scares you. There is virtually no roadblock or mountain you cannot circumvent. That allows for some huge business building. But it also opens the door for some significant collateral damage.

Think in terms of Builder/Opportunists like Sir Richard Branson and Donald Trump. This DNA combination creates the ultimate party boys and girls. They live with tons of glitz and glamour. But many could argue that even though they handle a disproportionate amount of wealth (relative to other BOSI DNAs), there may be other areas of their lives that are not thriving at the same level.

You need to take the time to study the weaknesses of both the Builder DNA and the Opportunist DNA. You need to also make sure to build your sensory muscle to alert you when your Builder DNA or Opportunist DNA is taking you into a danger zone of its weakness. The more you flex that sensory muscle to send the red alert, the savvier you will become at making decisions. More importantly, you'll build a more balanced business and life.

Here is a summary of what the Opportunist DNA in you will tend to do so that you can be aware when it is manifesting itself in your decision-making processes.

- Jump on every income opportunity that comes your way (fear of loss will be the driver pushing you to make impulsive decisions).
- Want to launch new products, divisions, and ventures all the time.
- Be optimistic, no matter what the circumstance.
- Want to sell the company ASAP in order to catch the next money-making wave.
- Be impulsive when it comes to hiring people, entering into partnerships, and getting out of them.
- Not care what the cost is in order to get to the next level of success (sometimes to a fault).

Innovator DNA

One of the rarest BOSI DNA combinations is the Builder DNA and the Innovator DNA or BI. Here's why. Builder DNA is typically found in experienced businessmen and women. They find it easy to start up and build companies. The Innovator, on the other hand, struggles with designing or deploying the step-by-step plan for business development. With that said, there are instances when an individual with a Builder DNA experiences guest appearances from the Innovator DNA during the entrepreneurial journey.

That does not mean the Innovator DNA should always win the battle with the Builder DNA. What it does mean is that when the Innovator DNA kicks in, you should give it due process. Since the Innovator DNA is cross-quadrant to the Builder, you'll end up picking up some incredible weakness-overcoming benefits along the way.

For example: When the Builder DNA in you wants to crush any dissenters, the Innovator DNA in you will have empathy with people. At the same time, the Innovator DNA in you will want to build high-quality products and deliver them to customers in a way that adds great value to their lives. Builder DNA will want to build for scale, no matter what. Innovator DNA will want to ensure a positive corporate culture, happy clients, and a general feeling of well-being for all. When your Builder DNA is tempted to cross the integrity line on a business deal, the Innovator DNA in you will raise the caution flag. When the Builder DNA in you is ready to walk away from a relationship, the Innovator DNA will work to mend it. When the Builder DNA calls for ruthless realism, the Innovator DNA will balance it with loving empathy.

Summary

If your primary DNA is Builder, focus on the strengths and growth areas of the Builder DNA. Then just be aware of how some of your Secondary DNAs pop their head up into your business and life. Being aware is 90 percent of the battle. Hopefully as early as this week, you'll find yourself thinking "Gosh, that must be the Opportunist in me talking!" In most cases, you'll just laugh off your Secondary DNA. But in some cases, you'll make a tactical move to compensate for a weakness of your Primary DNA or leverage the strength in one of your Secondary DNAs.

The Action Plan Checklist

Here is a quick action planner you can use to start the process of moving to deploy some of the strategies you have learned.

You may choose to skip one or more strategies because you have intuitively optimized them already.

Optimization Points	Priority (1-7)	Start Date	Resources/People Needed
Optimize Your Business Model			
Optimize Your Organizational Structure			
Optimize Your Business Development			
Optimize Your Financing and Exit Strategy			
Optimize Your Relationships			
Optimize Your Advisory Team			
Optimize Your Leadership Development Plan			

$$\left[\; \text{c h a p t e r} \;\right]$$

7

The Opportunist DNA: "Who Cares, Let's Do It"

We know by now that the quintessential Opportunist is the particular type of entrepreneur who is driven by a desire to acquire wealth quickly and live off the spoils of that wealth for the long-term. We'll return to our story from Chapter 1 to show you how to best structure your business to take advantage of the distinctive traits of the Opportunist DNA.

Overview

Omar Kelly is a professional multilevel marketer. His mission is financial freedom, and is currently involved in his third multilevel marketing (MLM) venture. He is doing quite well this time, despite some setbacks along the way. Omar also does Forex Trading every morning and is working with his bank on liquidating some investment properties he got stuck with when the 2008 real estate bubble burst.

Plug and Play

To me, one of the greatest things about computers is the invention of the USB port. I can plug in a printer, a phone, a keyboard, and dozens of other devices into a USB port and I'm ready to go. Plug and play. I love it!

When it comes to business, Omar is quite the same way. He loves systems that he can just plug into. Network marketing ventures, franchises, agencies, quick-flip real estate deals, Internet marketing software, and other money-making systems have great appeal. That's because Omar is not interested in reinventing the wheel.

Omar is convinced that making money is all about being at the right place at the right time. It's all about being there at the ground floor. You know the ones: "You put $1,000 in this week, and in six hours it's turned into this, and in six days, it's turned into some multiple of that, and in six months, it's just turned into $100,000!"

He gets pretty fired up about finding a piece of real estate that is selling for pennies on the dollar that he could buy, develop, and flip for a huge multiple. Omar's goal is to position himself well in a deal, work hard for a period of time, and then pull the plug, sit back, and enjoy a passive income stream forever.

The Natural Born Promoter

When Omar gets passionate about something, he turns into a promotional machine. He can't stop talking about it. For example, when he got involved with his first MLM company, he heard some anecdotal stories about the incredible results people were having with the company's product. Omar became an "evangelist." He felt he had to tell everyone about this revolutionary new product. Interestingly enough, the same scenario played out in other business ventures. Moments after Omar was introduced to his first quick-flip real estate deal, he was on the phone with his Rolodex of business contacts, letting them know how they could "get in" on the deal.

Being a promoter is in Omar's DNA. When he launched his entrepreneurial career, that promotional power yielded him some incredible results. His passion and excitement drew people in. Many jumped into business with him.

But now, several years into the journey, Omar has noticed that his influence with people is waning. They aren't jumping on everything he brings to the table. As a matter of fact, some people are to the point of avoiding his phone calls. That frustrates Omar. After all, *he's just trying to help enough people get what they want so he can get what he wants in life.*

"I'd Like a Taste of That, Too!"

It's interesting to walk into an ice cream store and watch people ordering. Guys like me walk right up to the counter and order two scoops of vanilla in a cone. Others, like my wife, stand in awe staring through the glass barrier at every conceivable flavor combination wondering which one to choose. No sooner does she make her choice of chocolate-something-something then she sees someone else with a more decadent selection. Wait! Did she really make the right choice or should she go with the incredible new discovery?

Omar has something in common with my wife's ice cream selection challenge. He picked business opportunity no.1 (the weight-loss MLM company). However, no sooner had the rubber hit the road on marketing that opportunity, than his upline Bill told him about business opportunity no. 2 (the online marketing system). A few weeks later, he was on a mastermind teleconference and was introduced to a real estate investment opportunity where he could get in for as little as $50,000 and walk away with as much as $600,000 once the landowner had secured "the deal" with a potential developer. But Omar would have to move quickly to get his position in the real estate investment.

Fear of loss drives Omar. This fear is so strong that he often cannot say no to whatever comes across his plate. This is the Achilles' heel of the Opportunist. Say no to a money-making deal? Just the thought of missing out on such a deal drives him nuts. What if someone else makes the money . . . *and he doesn't?*

"I Hate Homework"

Omar has an excellent work ethic. He is willing to work 18-hour days for a period of time to get to his goal of financial freedom. But interestingly enough, he doesn't apply that work ethic when it comes to doing due diligence on a "special offer." The excitement of the opportunity combined with the fear of loss of the opportunity drives him to make decisions without doing the proper homework. Knowing this about people like Omar, savvy marketers (especially those in information marketing) know how to hit Omar's hot buttons. They know that a catchy headline, a bunch of testimonials, an ironclad guarantee, and a limited-time offer get him involved almost every time. Sometimes these opportunities work out, and he makes a ton of money fast. But more times than not, Omar steps on land mines that he could have easily avoided.

"Why Isn't It Happening Yet?"

Omar's no. 1 frustration is the feeling that he is not reaching his goals fast enough. He was doing so well in his second MLM business, and things were going great, but suddenly things crashed and he was back at square one. For some reason, success doesn't seem to stick for him.

His wife Beth explains the situation this way: "Omar, what is happening is that you start having success in one thing, and then four other things come up, and you start moving your time, resources, and money into these other things to try and leverage these incomes, and create multiple streams of income." Right when his new venture needed him the most—when it hit the first growth wave and he needed to really focus—he was *diversifying*.

"If I Just Had an Infusion of Cash Right Now!"

Just a couple of months ago, Omar did find a good opportunity. But there was a challenge. No access to start-up capital!

Here's how that played out:

In the past, his excitement about some other once-in-a-lifetime opportunities led him to leverage his credibility to get funding from trusted sources. Friends, family, and Beth's 401-k were all willing participants. Omar tapped it all because he found "the one" that was going to work! But circumstances beyond Omar's control led those opportunities down the tube and his friends and family didn't get the return they were expecting. As a matter of fact, they lost tens of thousands of dollars.

One of the great things about Omar is his short-term memory. It's easy for him to forget a painful situation like that and eagerly move on to the next thing that comes along. When describing his latest gig he has been heard to say, "I know that was the one, but this is *really* the one!"

His friends and family have more long-term memories, though, and eventually Omar found that the well of capital he counted on had dried up. When the legitimate opportunity did come along, his past track record made it hard to go back to those people yet again.

How frustrating! He had paid his dues, made some mistakes, learned a lot . . . but now, when he needed it the most, the infusion of cash wasn't available.

The Puzzle Is Almost Complete

Omar doesn't know it yet, but his short-term memory toward challenges is actually one of his biggest strengths. He is able to brush off the bumps in the road quickly, and move on to something else with an optimistic view of the future. And remember, Omar also has an awesome work ethic. He is willing to give up tireless hours of his time, even hours of sleep, to work on something he believes in. Couple that work ethic with his short-term memory, and he really does have a lot of the key pieces of the puzzle to business success. Now all Omar needs to do is figure out how to identify and overcome the prewired weaknesses of his Entrepreneurial DNA and he will be one powerhouse of a businessperson.

High and Low Opportunist DNA

For purposes of our discussion over the next few pages, I want to introduce you to the concept of high and low Opportunist DNA.

Put simply, if you earned a high number of points on the BOSI Test for Opportunist DNA, you are high Opportunist DNA. If you earned a relatively lower number of points, consider yourself low Opportunist DNA.

Opportunist DNA at Work

Work is a necessary evil in the world of the Opportunist. It is simply a means to an end. Given the choice, Opportunists would much rather be sitting on a tropical beach sipping a mai tai than checking portfolio values from a smart phone. However, to get to that point in life, Opportunists know they have to get some work done.

Opportunists love being around like-minded, positive people. Environments rich in personal development, motivation (dare I say rah-rah), and huge incentives are very attractive to people with this DNA. Opportunists thrive in situations where there is a massive carrot on a stick and a relatively short timeline of execution; longer term opportunities do not pan out as well. Opportunists would much rather work hard for a few months to a couple of years than make a commitment of over five years to anything. When an Opportunist does find a venture he or she gets excited about, the Opportunist will "sell out" to that venture and give virtually everything he or she has.

Opportunist DNA at Home

Since an Opportunist finds it so easy to "sell out" to a venture, it leads to an interesting dynamic in a home environment. Family members can look back on the career of an entrepreneur with high Opportunist DNA and chart family time to find it looks like a sine wave with very high amplitudes. It is not uncommon to hear family members say the following when describing someone with Opportunist DNA: "She was doing fine for a while. Then she got excited about a new business she started and we almost didn't see her for the next 10 months."

It's sad to say, but I have seen this side of the Opportunist DNA rip families apart. Family members (especially spouses and children) who are unaware of the traits that drive an Opportunist can easily interpret an entrepreneur's passionate pursuit of success as a lack of love for *them*. Left unchecked, these feelings often grow into resentment and significant relational damage.

When Opportunists are not in the "zone" of getting rich quickly, they have a lot of fun in family environments. Entrepreneurs with Opportunist DNA love to socialize, eat out in big groups, travel, and essentially enjoy life. The family members of entrepreneurs with this DNA should learn to enjoy these times when Opportunist DNA is *not in* the zone—while allowing for bursts of activity when Opportunist DNA is *in* the zone. Meanwhile, if the entrepreneur him- or herself is fully aware of his or her tendency to abandon all else when focused on making money, he or she can make adjustments to be a better member of the family. When both sides work together to harness the strengths of this DNA while overcoming its weaknesses, the home of someone with Opportunist DNA can be a fun and positive environment.

Opportunist DNA at Its Best

Opportunists are at their best when they take a proven concept with established operating systems to market. Put another way, Opportunists are at their best when they are leveraging the systems built and managed by a Builder.

Why? Because a Builder typically takes the risks of start-up and headaches of operational management off the table. This allows an Opportunist to simply plug in, promote, and get rich. When you think in terms of most franchise, MLM, dealer, or agency organizations out there, the business is typically run by a Builder and marketed by an Opportunist.

The hand-in-glove relationship between Builders and Opportunists cannot be overstated. It is the formula that has built the largest corporations on the planet—and will continue to do so. But both the Builder and the Opportunist must understand each other better and recognize that the higher the level of Opportunist DNA, the shorter the stay with any given entity.

The desire to get to financial independence faster will always drive high Opportunist DNA entrepreneurs to seek greener pastures. The thrill of *never having to work again because they worked hard, made a pile of cash, and are now living off passive income* is what an Opportunist is all about it.

Opportunist DNA at Its Worst

Opportunist DNA is at its worst when it is left to its own resources to conjure up a business idea and take it to market. Don't get me wrong, an Opportunist comes up with some great ideas every once in a while. But the market successes of those ideas are often few and far between. A majority of the ideas generated by an Opportunist are driven by a desire to get rich fast, so they typically lack a more strategic market-based approach to product development. There are garages and storage facilities full of unsold product inventions and patent applications designed by Opportunists looking to sell millions of units of a "life-changing" product.

Individuals with low Opportunist DNA are often able to avoid the trap of starting up a venture from the ground up. They typically look to leverage the systems of an established brand to make money. Individuals with high Opportunist DNA, however, tend to have a bit of an ego and look to set off on their own long before they are ready to own or operate a business.

Ideal Business Ventures for Opportunists

There is a massive marketplace of opportunity for entrepreneurs with Opportunist DNA. I can safely say that this DNA has the largest pool of potential businesses to pick from. At the heart of any ideal venture for an Opportunist will be some sort of promotional or selling activity. Selling is what Opportunists are most gifted to do.

Most salespeople have Opportunist DNA in them. I will be so bold as to say that it is impossible to be a good salesperson without a decent amount of Opportunist DNA.

Here's why. These individuals have just enough Opportunist DNA to access the great strengths of this DNA (like positive mind-set, high work ethic, short-term memory on setbacks, passion for promoting, driven by incentives). Yet, they don't have too much Opportunist DNA to manifest some of its weaknesses (like impulsiveness, lack of long-term focus, procrastination, and laziness).

Businesses for Opportunists to Avoid

Start-ups are the no. 1 red flag for those with Opportunist DNA. If you have low Opportunist DNA, you should consider starting up a company *only* if you have partners who have Builder and/or Specialist DNA. They will do the things in the start-up that you are not gifted to do.

If you have high Opportunist DNA, I would strongly advise you against starting up your own company. The time, stress, and energy required to start up a venture will drive you absolutely insane. You may feel like a hot shot with the business card of "owner," "CEO," or "president," but you are simply not suited for the post. Your amazing gifts can be leveraged so much better in a venture that is already up and running. Don't waste your talent on a start-up.

Buying an existing business that was run by Specialist or a Builder is also a red flag for an Opportunist. Builder DNA entrepreneurs are very good at pitching Opportunists on why the Opportunist needs to beg, borrow, or steal to buy a business (or asset) owned by the Builder. Opportunist DNA, in its weakness, is quick to jump on the massive cash flows and value of the Builder's venture. Most often, under the Opportunist's watch, the venture or asset loses value. As an Opportunist, you are easily swayed, so you should beware of ventures and assets being sold by people who don't share your Entrepreneurial DNA.

Some yellow flag ventures for Opportunists are ones that have a very rigid job description or ones that come with a set of regulatory restrictions. An Opportunist becomes a caged panther when forced inside a box or made to sit in a cubicle. Evaluate the opportunity being offered to you carefully. If there are several management layers of decision making or if you will have to jump through too many hoops to get something done, there is a chance the fire in your belly will die quickly. The lower your Opportunist DNA, the less of a yellow flag this becomes.

Some Tips on Partnerships and Alliances

By nature, Opportunists tend to partner with other Opportunists. It's just so darn convenient. After all, birds of a feather flock together right?

But is that the optimal scenario for reaching your goals and dreams? As you read through this section, you have probably figured out that an Opportunist-Opportunist partnership, though fun, could simply accentuate weaknesses of the DNA and deter success. With that said, I have seen many situations where two Opportunists partnered together have done fairly well. The primary takeaway value of this partnership is the sheer camaraderie and support that comes from being in business with a like-minded individual.

But there are a couple of better options. They may not be as "easy" interpersonally, but I can assure you, they typically work out to be more profitable for all involved.

Specialist DNA Partnered with Opportunist DNA

It goes without saying that a cross-quadrant partnership has its benefits. After all, the strengths of the Specialist DNA offset the weaknesses of the Opportunist DNA. Refer back to my comments on having Secondary Specialist DNA, in the previous chapter, and you'll see how those differences play out.

I am reminded of an American Express TV commercial where one partner (the face man/sales guy) is on the road calling in the results of his road trip to his business partner (the brew master) back home. Each call comes with more good news of sales of their micro brew to bars and pubs around the world. "We're going to need more equipment," says the happy Specialist partner. Meanwhile, the happy Opportunist partner is traveling the globe doing what he loves.

That same scenario plays itself out successfully all over the world. When an IT guy (Specialist DNA) teams up with a sales guy (Opportunist DNA), the two can build a very successful company together. The sales guy can focus on landing new accounts and keeping the cash register ringing. The IT guy can focus on servicing the customer and managing the office environment.

A cross-quadrant partnership will also have its tough days. Yin-yang relationships have their ups *and* downs. It is imperative for one of the partners to have the final say in the business so as to avoid stalemates and drawn out sessions of mental gymnastics. I have found that partnerships where the Specialist has the majority interest perform better for the long term than those where the Opportunist has the final decision.

Builder DNA Partnered with Opportunist DNA

A healthy Builder-Opportunist partnership is a sight to behold in the marketplace. These two DNAs work well to generate massive market results (albeit with significant interpersonal challenges).

I've mentioned it before, but it bears repeating. A Builder's ability to create highly scalable systems and brands just makes it easier for Opportunist DNA to take that brand to the marketplace with a big bang. When an Opportunist is teamed up with a Builder, the sky is the limit on growth and income generation. It's worth repeating again that every franchise, MLM, agency, and dealer organization is essentially the partnership of a Builder and an Opportunist. The results speak for themselves.

As an individual with Opportunist DNA you just have to know that all this success and upside comes with a price. Builders will want to dominate and control every conversation, situation, and decision. If you are willing to let the Builder "win" most of the time, you will have a prosperous journey. If you can figure out how to make your Builder partner "feel" like he or she won, even though you know you got what you wanted, then consider yourself miles ahead of the pack.

Some Typical Statements Made by an Opportunist

If you have made any of these statements, you have been exhibiting Opportunist tendencies. Given your new knowledge about your Entrepreneurial DNA, think about these for a few minutes and see how they fit with your business.

- I love the idea of working hard for a window of time (two to five years) making a fortune, and then living the life thereafter.
- I have been involved in multiple business ventures at the same time.
- I am surrounded by dream stealers. Some of them are the people closest to me.
- If the right people would just invest in this business venture with me, it would be a huge success.
- I don't mind working 18 hours a day for a window of time if I can enjoy the benefits for the rest of my life.
- I am an optimist through and through. Despite the occasional failure along the way, I am confident I am going to strike it *big* on my current venture.
- I have a hard time saying no to money-making opportunities—especially the ones that don't take a lot of ongoing time.

BOSI BUSINESS STRATEGY ALERT!

Do you have an advisory board that has the ability to say no to business opportunities for you? If not, you will end up making impulsive decisions that will continue to keep you from reaching your goal of financial freedom.

- I am always open to looking at ways to develop wealth by working "smarter, not harder."
- I laugh in the face of risk. The riskier, the higher the payout potential—so bring it on.
- I could never, ever work at a *job* or run a repetitive business for the long term.
- I like finding deals where the timing is just right (ground floor), the right people are in place, and all I have to do is jump in and ride the wave.
- I'd much rather earn residual/royalty income or some sort of dividend payout than go to an office everyday to earn a living.
- I have one or more business ventures that have failed, but I am now building in a totally different industry.
- I find it hard to focus on just one business opportunity/system for any sustained period of time.
- If someone brings me a stock tip or guaranteed income opportunity, I'll say yes a majority of the time.
- I've burned some financial bridges with people because I promoted a financial opportunity that failed.
- Flipping real estate, MLM, day trading, franchise ownership, investing in Forex, eBay selling . . . I've tried most all of those.

BOSI BUSINESS STRATEGY ALERT!

You are willing to go out of balance on work-life issues in order to achieve your goal of financial independence. But what impact is that having on those closest to you? While you are out there landing the big fish, what is the collateral damage at home?

- I am very coachable, especially when I'm dealing with a top income earner in my field.
- I enjoy personal development. I don't care what the cost is if I can be mentored by the best in the business.

- A great lifestyle doing what I really love (family time, volunteering, etc.) is more important to me than a stable paycheck.
- I will be financially independent in two to five years if things go according to plan.
- I will beg, borrow, and steal to get in on a business opportunity that makes sense.
- I can absolutely see the venture I am being part of a billion-dollar entity in the next few years.
- I love being around like-minded, positive people.
- I'd rather leverage an existing high-growth business trend or brand than have to start and operate one of my own.

The Opportunist DNA at a Glance

STRENGTHS	WEAKNESSES	FRUSTRATIONS
Opportunists have a very high work ethic when focused on a particular venture. 10- to 18-hour days don't scare the Opportunist in the least.	Saying no to opportunities is very hard. This has and will continue to cost the Opportunist money, time, and headaches if left unchecked.	Financial freedom can be a moving target. Just when the Opportunist feels he or she has landed the big fish, it gets away.
Being optimistic towards life allows the Opportunist to shake off short-term setbacks. This gives him or her significant market advantage against those who are more *realistic* or *pessimistic*.	Doing due diligence on an opportunity feels worse than a root canal. The Opportunist sees analytical people as "slow" and "closed-minded."	Dream stealers and negative people just suck the life out of the Opportunist. Unfortunately many of these naysayers happen to be the people closest to the Opportunist.
Opportunists are very coachable, especially when they enter a new industry. They seek out the top producers and learn from them.	They tend to juggle too many income opportunities at any given time. It is hard for them to pick one venture and focus on it exclusively.	Access to capital can be tricky especially when a large amount of money is needed.

chapter

8

Seven Business Optimization Strategies for Opportunist DNA

Opportunist DNA gives you a compelling set of gifts that can be leveraged in the marketplace. We learned about those unique strengths in the previous chapter. But we also learned about some compelling weaknesses. This chapter is designed to give you some *actionable strategy* on how to leverage your innate strengths while compensating for your potential weaknesses. Think of it as an optimization process. In some cases, we will be fixing something that is broken. In other cases, we will be taking proactive and precautionary strategies. In a couple of areas, we may not have to do a thing! You may have intuitively taken the necessary optimization steps already.

Being involved in a venture that isn't well-suited for your Entrepreneurial DNA is going to be a very frustrating situation for you. So will not having a plan that is optimized to your unique strengths and weaknesses. The seven strategies we will be discussing in this chapter are designed to make sure you achieve your goals and dreams faster and safer than before. The seven strategies we'll discuss are:

- Optimize Your Business, Part 1: Build versus Leverage
- Optimize Your Business, Part 2: Going "All In"
- Optimize Your Team, Part 1: Your Advisory Board
- Optimize Your Team, Part 2: Your Coach
- Optimize Your Credibility
- Optimize Your Work-Life Balance Plan
- Optimize Your Personal Leadership Development Plan

Strategy One—Optimize Your Business, Part 1: Build versus Leverage

This is really a matter of your business model. If you scored fairly high as an Opportunist (O) in the BOSI Test, I must make a very strong recommendation to you: Don't start up your own business. You are not built to start up and grow a company for the long term. Remember the story in Chapter 2 where Kendal tested me on that OmegaWave device. He told me that even though I *thought* I was a soccer player, I really wasn't built to be one.

If you scored high as an Opportunist in the BOSI Test, you have some amazing gifts. But dealing with the headaches of starting and running a business is not one of them. Opportunists are much better at leveraging existing money-making systems. That's why they thrive in industries like multilevel marketing (MLM), online marketing, franchising, real estate, and professional sales. The system is already in place; all the Opportunist has to do is plug in and do what he or she does best—which is *promote*.

Opportunists also make great passive investors. After all, you're not looking to get your hands dirty. You just want to use high-potential businesses as a vehicle to get to your goal. So do what comes naturally to you. If you do have plans to operate your own company (or already do operate your own company), you will find that having a business partner with left-quadrant DNA (Builder, Specialist) will be a massive asset.

In 2003, I had a chance to work with one of the most well-known NFL players of all time. He had an idea for a financial services start-up and my name came up on the radar as someone who could help him get it off the ground. Keep in mind, this is well before I discovered Entrepreneurial DNA. I know now that he is pretty close to a purebred Opportunist.

I will shorten the story and tell you what a painful experience it was to watch him try to force himself to start up his own company. We wrote the business plan and even raised some money with his friends and family. Some of the biggest corporations on earth came to the table to build technology and provide their expertise. It was an entrepreneur's dream come true. But it wasn't his. He was showing up at an office he didn't want to be in. He was dealing with management issues he didn't like. He was sitting in four-hour meetings that felt worse than any hit he took in the NFL.

Six months into the launch of the company, he had lost interest in the venture and been recruited to half a dozen other deals. The truth is, he was happier doing those other deals. And he made more money there!

That's my point. Why put yourself in a position of discomfort when you can be just as successful doing what you were gifted to do?

The bottom line? If you have high Opportunist DNA, don't build your own company. Invest your time, money, and talent into someone else's company. Builder and Specialist companies are excellent places for you to create leverage and keep the lifestyle you love.

Now if you had a pretty even Opportunist-Builder (OB) or Opportunist-Specialist (OS) in your BOSI Profile, then you may be okay pursuing your own ground-up operation. But 9 times out of 10, I'd say ... "leverage."

Here is one more story I will share with you to make the point from a personal and very painful growth experience. In 1999 I met a dynamic and charismatic entrepreneur who decided to take me under his wing and teach me the ropes in business.

I was so enamored by his personality, promotional capability, and leadership skills that I was instantly drawn to work with him. Had I known then what I know now, I would have instantly profiled him as *very* high Opportunist DNA. Based on that, I would have still worked with him but I would have done so in a totally different capacity. Unfortunately back then I didn't know any better. To me, he was just a great guy with a ton of great ideas.

Those "great ideas" were quickly spun into business ventures. First, there was the lead generation company. Then, we started up a sales training company that would help our lead buyer customers get better results. Within a few months, my business mentor saw the opportunity to start a sales-force automation company that would help those lead buyer customers (who were now well trained) get even better results with automated follow-up.

As if that wasn't enough, he went on a weekend getaway in 2001 to Las Vegas only to return home and notify us that we were also going to start a travel company. (The guy who sat next to him in first class had some great insider travel deals to offer him.)

Don't get me wrong. Back in those days, I was pumped! I was so excited to be part of such a dynamic business incubator. I was placed in charge of the sales-force automation company. That company grew to over 20,000 customers in 18 months. We were growing and making money hand over fist. But here was the problem. My mentor lacked the balance of Builder DNA that would allow him to handle multiple start-ups at the same time. He jumped from idea to idea with no standard operating procedures, systems, or financing strategy in place. Instead of surrounding himself with seasoned advisors and experts who could guide him, he hired a bunch of young entrepreneurial types like us—people who thought he was the expert in everything.

Soon it all started to unravel. His focus shifted to the next venture (and the one after that). Meanwhile the incubated companies that had been started up were struggling for air, leadership, and financial support. Before I knew it, the corporate account I was responsible for became the slush fund for his next great idea.

The staff that was supposed to be working for one company was suddenly working for the "next great idea" he had.

That experience taught me more than I can ever describe to you. I am still grateful to him for having taught me the things he had. Much of what you are reading in this book came from the experiences in that incubator. However, that experience was also costly.

Two years after I left his team to start my own company, I started getting letters from individuals and agencies letting me know that he had decided to move on without fulfilling his seven-figure financial obligations and my name was next in line to facilitate. Hundreds of thousands of dollars in payments and a bankruptcy later, I sit here penning these words.

Listen to me my friend. If you have a high Opportunist DNA, please seriously reconsider running your own company. There is much more you will be putting to risk than your own fame and fortune. If this book didn't catch you early enough in the game—and you are running your own company, let me make a different strong recommendation. Engage a business partner with Builder DNA and/or Specialist DNA to hand off the operational control and oversight. If a business partner is not in the cards, then hire a full time CEO to run the company and get yourself out of the role of making the strategic and financial decisions for the company. Instead, put yourself in the position of making the business development, marketing, and promotional decisions of the company. That is where you will see the best ROI for your time and passion.

I'll conclude this strategy by restating my core point. If you have high Opportunist DNA, leverage someone else's infrastructure and make a ton of money doing what you are gifted at.

Strategy Two—Optimize Your Business, Part 2: Going "All In"

It doesn't matter if it is a network-marketing opportunity, real estate venture, day-trading system, franchise location, an online marketing project, or anything else. **Pick one business venture and make the commitment to see it through for the next 24 to 36 months.** Now, when I say pick *one* business venture and make the commitment to see it through, I mean "forsaking all others until death do you part."

This is going to require some soul-searching on your part to pick through the various ventures you may have on your plate and choose *only one*. So just for fun, let's do a quick experiment. Ready?

If I were to offer you a million dollars to drop everything and just focus on one business venture for the next 24 to 36 months, which one of your ventures would you keep? Do you have the one? Great, we've just completed Strategy Two. You have the venture you are going to focus on for the next window of time. Dump the rest, pronto.

"But Joe, you don't understand, I have money and time tied up in those other ventures and I literally just have to sit back and wait to get paid for a couple of them," you say.

Dump 'em anyway. Get them out of your mind and consciousness.

"But Joe, what about multiple streams of income? Don't you know that the real millionaires out there have multiple streams of income?" you ask.

Okay, you asked for it, let me put that whole multiple income streams discussion to bed once and for all. The truth about multiple streams of income is this. Contrary to the mumbo jumbo about "multiple streams of income" being promoted by information marketers and business opportunity sellers, it is not what you may think it is. In reality, multiple streams of income is an *end goal of having built* wealth. It is not the *means* to wealth.

Maybe you heard some multimillionaire guru talk about his or her multiple streams of income and his or her wonderful stress-free life. You may have jumped out of your chair to say, "I want that!"

However, here's the part of the story you may have subconsciously (or very consciously) skipped. That multimillionaire who today has multiple streams of income started with *one* income stream. That's right. He or she started with one, focused on it, built it up to a level of success, and reinvested those profits to add on income stream number two, and then eventually income stream numbers three and four.

Don't get me wrong, I can see the appeal of mailbox money. The only thing better than mailbox money is mailbox money from multiple sources. However, I have yet to meet someone who has developed true wealth by focusing on multiple income streams at the same time. I've worked with a lot of Opportunists who had a "day job" and an entrepreneurial venture on the side. That's okay in my book. However, it's when you have your day job, plus the entrepreneurial venture, plus, plus, plus, that you virtually guarantee your demise.

I recognize that I am asking you to do something that sounds almost insane on the surface. I can almost hear your brain short-circuit as you seriously ponder the decision to walk away from deals you are already invested in. I was in the exact same boat several years ago myself. I would simply ask you to put this mission-critical strategy to the test for 24 months—no more, no less. Two years from now, evaluate your market position, personal income, and goals. You will not be disappointed.

I have friends who, because of their Opportunist gifting, have generated as much as $200,000 in income in one weekend. Those friends could have sustained those results (or something close to it) for years and years—if they had just focused. But they didn't. No sooner had the money hit the bank account then they had found a way to parlay that money to make $2 million. But they didn't make the $2 million—and they were back on the road and starting over again.

If you are not yet a multimillionaire, stop everything. Commit to one entrepreneurial venture and do just that one project until you are successful at it. *Then* consider adding on venture number two. If you shortcut this step, you are setting yourself up for a world of hurt.

Pick one, dump the rest. You'll be glad you did.

Strategy Three—Optimize Your Team, Part 1: Your Advisory Board

If you are taking Strategy Two seriously, you are going to need help and support to get through the process. As we have learned in our time together, your BOSI DNA's greatest weakness is your inability to say "no" when a tempting offer comes your way. Take it from me, a guy who gets presented great money-making opportunities every single day. It's hard to say no on your own. If you have any intention of reaching your goal of financial freedom in the next two to five years, you must counter your impulsive side with an objective group of advisors.

With the BOSI Quadrant in mind, I'd like to recommend that you go through your Rolodex and find three to five very seasoned individuals who have BOSI Profiles that *differ* from yours. There is no point surrounding yourself with a bunch of yes people who will want to jump into every money-making deal *with* you. Ideally, your Advisory Board will include one or two Builders (people who have built very successful companies in more than one industry). Then add in a couple of Specialists. Think of attorneys, CPAs, financial planners, and graphic designers. (You know the people who run those businesses you think are utterly "boring"? Yes, you will need two of them on your Advisory Board).

If you can find someone with Innovator DNA, that's great, but an Innovator typically won't add a whole lot of value to your business needs. The bottom line is that you need Builder and Specialist DNAs on your Advisory Board. If you need some help, use the free relationship analyzer tools available in the BOSI online community and optimize your Advisory Board from there.

"Wow, Joe, I'm not going to do this crazy step," you say. "I have to work pretty hard to stay away from these *dream-stealing no-vision-having cynics*. I'm not going to have them advise me. I'll do this one on my own."

Oh, really? How's that going for you so far?

Trust me when I tell you, this is the defining difference between *successful* Opportunists and *struggling* Opportunists. Some of my closest friends have tons of Opportunist DNA and the ones that have built an optimized Advisory Board have stayed out of trouble. They have made money faster and they are closer to their goals than ever before. The Opportunists who skip this strategy make a ton of money for six months to a year and then lose it all, and then start the cycle all over again.

Now here is what you do with your Advisory Board prospect list. Ask them to be part of your Advisory Board. Their only obligation is to evaluate any and all business opportunities and decisions that come your way and advise you on your involvement. That is it. They do not have to check in with you every week or every month. They do not have to babysit your finances (or know anything about your finances). You just give them the full authority in your life to *vote for or against* your involvement in a business venture. If they vote yes, go for it. If they vote no, walk away. It's that simple.

If your Advisory Board does not hear from you for a whole year, that's okay. It just means that you have not considered a new business venture in that long (if you're being honest, they'll hear from you, though). The goal of this Advisory Board is for people, who are not like you, to help you slow the process of jumping into a venture to a pace where wiser, discerning decisions can be made. They will help you avoid a lot of lost money, time, and heartache. An advisory board is a critical part of your success journey.

I know that I am giving you some pretty tough pills to swallow. I promise that it gets easier from here. I can also assure you that the results you will see from Strategies Two and Three will be *game changing* for you and your business.

Strategy Four—Optimize Your Team, Part 2: Your Coach

A coach is going to pick up where your Advisory Board leaves off. Let's say you've completed Strategy Two and Strategy Three. That means you're actively involved in a safe, long-term business venture that has been vetted by people who are *not* like you. Now it is time to make sure that someone is going to keep you accountable to put the blinders on and stay focused on the tasks that need to take place for you to achieve your long-term mission.

Rather than attend 15 seminars on how to be more focused, just engage a coach who can help you do it at a very personalized, hands-on level. A good coach will make the process almost effortless and you will not have to go and "learn" something that you are not built to do. You should plan on a monthly investment of $300 to $800, depending on the type of business you operate. If you're not willing to make that investment, then you really should not be in business. Even if you have not earned $1 in your new venture, set aside the funds to have a seasoned coach advise and guide you through the business journey.

I have watched the coaching industry absolutely explode over the last three to four years. Today anybody with a Web site and a fancy logo is calling him- or herself a coach. There are even franchised coaching companies that will give the "business coach" title to anyone with $75,000 in his or her pocket. Make sure to screen your potential coach to make sure that he or she is not just someone who is going to pump you up every month. Also make sure that he or she has the business pedigree to truly advise you. Do some strong due diligence on the potential coach. Don't just go with what the LinkedIn Profile or blog bio says. Evaluate his or her Entrepreneurial DNA. Talk to a minimum of five past and current clients. Make sure the chemistry is right and that you respect him or her enough to let him or her coach you even when you don't like what he or she has to say. You want to find a coach who is going to help you solve challenges, make savvy decisions, and get things done in the marketplace.

Based on my extensive experience with Opportunists, I am convinced that a coach is a *must-have*. There are free tools on the BOSI Web site that will help you screen and vet your potential business coach.

Strategy Five: Optimize Your Credibility

Chances are, if you have been around the entrepreneurial world long enough, you have stubbed your toe a few times. As we discussed in a previous chapter, you may have even helped some people close to you stub *their* toes as well. That has probably put a damper on your credibility. If that is the case for you, you have a couple of options.

- **Option 1:** Ignore the matter and hope that it goes away.
- **Option 2:** Do something intentional to rebuild your lost credibility.

I don't know about you, but Option 2 sounds a lot better to me. It is definitely more work and it may sting a bit, but you and I both know, it is the better way. So here's how to go about rebuilding any lost credibility.

Have five people closest to you (ideally those who have paid a price for your entrepreneurial journey), take the "Perception Quiz" available for free at the BOSI Web site. Give each individual a copy of the quiz and ask him or her for candid answers to each question. If you want really objective and honest feedback, sign up at www.SurveyMonkey.com and create the quiz online. This way, your respondents can take the quiz anonymously.

As the quiz data comes back to you, review it with an open mind. Don't get offended, defensive, or reactive. Just take the input for what it is—feedback. Then take this feedback and use it to craft your mini-executive summary.

Write a two- or three-page executive summary that talks about your goal of financial freedom. Describe why you are pursuing this goal. Talk about the business venture you have chosen that is going to get you to that goal. Introduce the reader to your Advisory Board and describe each board member's business background. Talk about why the Advisory Board has approved the business venture you are in. Write about the coach that you have hired and what you and your coach have set out to do in the near term and in the long term.

Now give each of your survey respondents a copy of your executive summary. Show them that you have learned from your experiences, both good and bad, and you are now embarking on a new chapter of your success journey. Don't worry about their initial reaction to the document. If you do your job right, they will be taking back any negative comments within 36 months.

The reason it is important for you to go through this process is simple. I've worked with a lot of Opportunists who have said, "I'll just work really hard and get rich, and then everyone who didn't believe in me will eat their words and come groveling back." I have *never* seen that plan work.

These are your friends and your family. Engage them in the process of your growth, rather than alienate them. Even if they don't buy in right away, they'll see that something is different about your modus operandi.

You will have stepped out of the weakness of your Entrepreneurial DNA and into its gifting. They'll see the results of your work ethic, optimism, passion, and promotional strengths. Meanwhile, your Advisory Board and coach will help you accomplish things you have never accomplished before. Over time, some of the so-called "dream stealers" from your past will turn into your biggest cheerleaders. More importantly, they will be there to support you emotionally and join you financially when the time comes.

Strategy Six: Optimize Your Work-Life Balance Plan

The fact is, if you are not making a concerted effort to become healthier every day, you are wasting your time trying to be financially free. Chances are you have told yourself. "As soon as I get to income level X, I'm going to buy that expensive workout equipment and that spa membership and get healthy." That is a great goal for your dream-building wall and long-term vision casting, but you must engage in your health *now*.

If you do not, you could easily end up on five to 10 prescription medications, or have to have several surgeries, or even have a heart attack, and be a miserable millionaire. Let me state that just taking nutritional supplements is *not* a wellness journey. Wellness is about good lifestyle choices including diet, exercise, and rest. The journey of health doesn't have to be cumbersome, inconvenient, or painful. It's just a matter of simple, daily steps that will help you become a more effective and powerful entrepreneur.

Health also comes from a good work-life balance. Unfortunately for your work-life balance, you may be really excited about your current venture. You have convinced yourself that you have got to work like crazy to take advantage of the unique timing of the current venture. After all, there's the possibility of increased competition around the corner. As a result, you may be working insane hours knowing that very soon, if you do it right, you'll be able to pull the plug and enjoy lots of free time with your family, friends, and your soon-to-be-hired butler.

The fact is that you need to develop a comprehensive work-life balance plan that schedules in time for rest, relaxation, family, and spirituality *now*. Without it, you are wasting your time building your venture. You'll get rich, but you'll be a miserable, grumpy, and lonely rich person. Remember, your family and friends may not have totally bought in to your vision yet. You'll alienate them further by overdoing the business-building thing.

Now I have heard every excuse and rationalization in the book from Opportunists on why they must make sacrifices now for a pay-off later. That's hogwash and I'm not buying it. Developing work-life balance is as easy as scheduling some simple activities into your daily/weekly schedule and treating them with the same priority level as a business meeting or an investor presentation. Start small. Set some goals. Have your coach and mastermind team hold you accountable for the execution of your work-life balance plan. You'll be amazed at how much faster you reach your goals and dreams.

Strategy Seven: Optimize Your Personal Leadership Development Plan

I don't have a lot of "Joe-isms" out there, but here is one that I coined a long time ago. I hope this saying is one that sticks with you for the long term.

"They say entrepreneurship isn't brain surgery. I say it is brain surgery. It is brain surgery you do on yourself—without the anesthesia."

Success in business is a combination of mastering the "why" (personal development) and the "how" (business strategy). The personal development side of the equation is your "leadership journey."

The big breakthrough for me personally was to discover that Entrepreneurial DNA drives one's leadership journey just as much as it drives business strategy. If you, for example, try and follow the same leadership journey as someone with Builder DNA or Specialist DNA, you'll find yourself uninspired and quite frustrated. You'll notice that individuals with those DNAs have a completely different set of needs at the leadership level. For Opportunist DNA, there are three main areas of leadership development: Integrity, Vision and Mission, and Decision Matrix.

Area 1: Integrity

Integrity is a big word. Unfortunately it is also a word that is thrown around quite flippantly by people in the marketplace. Politicians claim they have integrity. Wall Street power-broker brands say they live by it. Pastors use it as a calling card. But what does *integrity* really mean and why is it an area of development for Opportunist DNA? Put simply, *integrity* means to "tell the truth and do what you promise."

That is a very, very hard thing for Opportunist DNA to do in many circumstances. Don't get me wrong. Opportunist DNA has the best of intentions when making a claim or a promise. However, Opportunist DNA often has to struggle with competing agendas. On one side there is the desire to serve people, be fair, and be truthful. On the other side there is the overwhelming desire to make money. In some cases, the opportunity to make money falls perfectly in line with serving people fairly and truthfully. Sometimes though, there is a conflict.

Here's a real-life example of this point. When I was a young entrepreneur, Opportunist DNA flowed through my system quite freely and without any interruption. During that window of time, I was involved in the network-marketing industry and doing quite well. But here was the conflict. On one side, I had the need to market the products and business opportunity to as many people as possible, as fast as possible. On the other side, I had come to learn that there was a specific profile of a successful network marketer. Put simply, I had learned that "credibility," "charisma," and "confidence" were three traits that were mission-critical for someone to achieve success in the marketplace. Unfortunately, most of the people I was presenting the opportunity to did not have that profile when I met them.

So that was the rub. "Should I sell them on the opportunity and make an extra buck or should I save them a ton of money and heartache?"

Some variation of that scenario crosses the mind of every salesperson and business owner at several points in a given day or week. I have found that the higher the Opportunist DNA, the easier it is to go for the extra buck.

Oh sure, it is easy to justify the decision as perfectly pure and good-hearted. Opportunist DNA is excellent at justifying anything it does. However, when the decision process is slowed down or discussed with an optimized mastermind group, the output usually comes out quite different.

Here's another example of how this issue plays out in real life. You're excited about a new venture. Let's assume it is an investment opportunity. The person who pitched you on the venture gave you what appeared to be some very compelling facts and figures about the venture. Right after you decide to engage with the venture then you find yourself promoting it to others around you. Of course, as part of that pitch, you find yourself parroting the facts and figures you heard previously. But here is the interesting part. The facts and figures you are parroting are just a bit sexier and "improved" than the original article. So if the original facts claimed that *one* guy had made a 20-times return, your facts may show that *many* people were making a 20-times return. If the original facts claimed that the company had filed *one provisional* patent, your recollection and explanation could be that the company had secured *a series of rock-solid* patents.

You see where I am going with this. Opportunist DNA (when left unchecked) will drive you to do almost anything to make money. It will even go as far as to willingly fabricate facts while making you, the entrepreneur, feel you are doing the best possible thing for mankind.

Relative to the other BOSI DNAs, telling the whole truth and following through on promises are growth areas for Opportunists. If you are living in victory in this area, consider yourself blessed. You have probably spent quite a bit of time and energy mastering this area of your life. If you do find yourself struggling in this area, then make the conscious decision to engage in an ongoing process of development and improvement to gain mastery over this area. Your business will be the better for it.

Remember the analogy I gave you earlier in this book about the angel and devil on your shoulder every time you are making a decision. There are times when Opportunist DNA is the angel on your shoulder—telling you to take a good risk, keep a positive outlook, work hard, and get results. However, there are times when Opportunist DNA is the devil on your shoulder too. The instinct to compromise integrity for a quick buck is one of those times.

Area 2: Vision and Mission

Opportunists like to fly by the seat of their pants and don't like to be fettered in any way. As a result, very little time and focus goes into mapping out a strategic plan for business and following it diligently. After all, a great new opportunity could pop up first thing tomorrow morning, right?

When I study the highly successful Opportunist DNA entrepreneurs out there, one of the defining differences between them and their counterparts is their strategic plan. They actually *have* one. Sir Richard Branson is a great example of an individual with Opportunist DNA who has a vision and mission that has allowed him to become one of the most successful entrepreneurs in the world. Do you have a strategic plan like his?

A *strategic plan* is simply an action plan that comes out of knowing one's *vision* (where you want to go in life) and one's *mission* (how you are going to get there). Discovering one's vision and mission is not a 10-minute hand-scribbled "back of a paper napkin" exercise. It takes introspection and process. I have included a complete strategic planning process in Chapter 13 of this book. I recommend that you begin the process and discipline of discovering your vision by mapping out your 36-month mission. Not only will it keep you from getting distracted, it will give you a significant feeling of focus and accomplishment along the way.

Area 3: Decision Matrix

One of the most powerful tools in your toolbox will be something I call a "decision matrix." Think of it as a series of filters you use when making a decision. Left to your own resources, as an Opportunist, you will have one single decision filter: Could the decision result in making lots of money fast? If yes, green light. If no, red light.

As you can imagine, that should not be the only decision filter in your toolbox. Now I am sure you have already installed other filters. The lower your Opportunist DNA score, the more filters you already have. Mastering the use of those filters is a huge driver of success for your DNA.

Start by spending some time looking at your core belief systems. What do you believe at your core about things like money, success, work, family, faith, work, retirement, wealth, your time, and talents?

If you take the time to journal some notes on your beliefs related to each of these major areas of life, you may be surprised to see the results. Many times, we get caught up following the "success formula" of another individual with values and core beliefs that are very *different* than ours. I certainly did.

This exercise will allow you to discover areas of your life where you are compromising your own core values in order to achieve success. Opportunist DNA is notorious for getting people to do that. This exercise will automatically start to create filters in your mind that will pop up to compete with any weakness of your Entrepreneurial DNA.

For example, let's say you decide that "quality of life with family" is a very important core value to you. You journal out some thoughts to find that it is actually a really big deal to you. The next time some guru on stage puts the hard court press on giving up family time or a certain quality of life with your family for a longer-term payoff, a decision filter will pop up like a red flag to say, "Hey! Don't forget about your core value commitment to family."

As an added benefit, these filters will reinforce strengths of your Entrepreneurial DNA and push you to make decisions that will move you closer to your vision and mission. Just as important, these new decision filters will help you build even stronger integrity.

Are you starting to see why I make the claim that when it comes to leadership development, one size doesn't fit all? If you have been following a one-size-fits-all leadership journey, dismount from that horse and engage in programming that is specifically built for your DNA.

Final Words about the Seven Strategies

So there we have it—seven areas in which you can dive in and optimize your entrepreneurial journey based on who you are built to be. Pay extra-close attention to Strategies One, Two and Three. That is where you will see the most significant return on investment (ROI) for your time, attention, and resources.

Factoring in Your Secondary DNAs

Chances are, you have a Builder, Specialist, or Innovator Secondary DNA. You may even have a combination of two or even three of them as your Secondary DNA. With that in mind, here are some important things you will need to be aware of when it comes to executing the seven strategies that I've just presented.

Builder DNA

Wow! That's all I can say if you are an Opportunist with some Builder DNA in you. You'll understand why as we get through this section together. Opportunist-Builders tend to build some of the fastest-growing, high-energy companies in the world. That's because they lack any filter of fear when it comes to pulling the trigger on action. The Opportunist DNA in you will want to soar to the highest heights and reach for the stars. The Builder DNA in you will figure out how to get it done. That's the power of the Opportunist-Builder. You possess limitless vision and business-building capacity to match. That's the good side of the equation.

Now for the not-so-good side of the equation. If you possess this DNA combination, you are a top or upper quadrant entrepreneur. Any time you find yourself heavy in a specific quadrant (be it upper, lower, left, or right), you can automatically expect blind spots and risk factors. Here are yours:

1. **People:** You will have the tendency to use people (the Builder DNA) and not slow down to fix the damage (the Opportunist DNA). You have to be extra careful with your personal and business relationships. Make sure to study the Builder DNA in this book to learn more about this topic.

2. **Overpromotion:** The Opportunist in you will tend to over-promote (some people call it hype or even B.S.). Truthfully, it goes back to our point from the earlier discussion about integrity. If you have $0.83 in your pocket, you could easily lead people to believe you have $830.00. If you just got back from staying the night at a three-star hotel, you could make people think you just stayed at the Taj Mahal. When a prospect asks you when a product could be delivered if it was purchased today, you most certainly would give the most aggressive timeline known to man. How am I doing so far?

The Builder DNA in you *enables* the overpromotional part of your Opportunist DNA, and that makes things more dangerous. The Builder in you may have actually pulled off a few magic tricks along the way. The prospect that wanted the product delivered on an incredibly tight timeline probably got the product delivered on schedule . . . once. That's because the Builder in you figured out how to keep up with the Opportunist in you. But just be aware that one-time feat gets etched in the Opportunist's mind and sets a new watermark for future overpromotion.

3. **An Obsession for Business:** There is a significant trend amongst individuals carrying the Opportunist-Builder DNA to make business (and its pursuit) the defining identity of his or her life. You will have a tendency to eat, sleep, and dream business. You probably find it very hard to be in a social environment and not talk about business. You struggle to keep business out of the conversation with friends and family. If truth be told, you get totally and utterly bored when any topic other than business is on the table.

   The business engine in your brain never turns off. Between the new and exciting ideas of the Opportunist DNA and the system-building, problem-solving mind of the Builder, the virtual lab in your brain runs at full capacity 24/7. I would call this the textbook definition of "obsessed." As a matter of fact, I looked it up. Webster's calls it "to haunt or excessively preoccupy the mind."

   Here's the point (and I think you know it already): With obsession comes imbalance. Anything that excessively preoccupies the mind will by nature displace other important things. These important things include:

   • Quality, private time with your spouse
   • Undistracted time with your children
   • A focus on your personal health and wellness
   • Service of others around you.

I have a Rolodex full of Builder-Opportunists who lost all the important things in their lives because they were unable to overcome this fatal flaw in their DNA. Like I've said all through this book, my goal is to just bring things to the forefront so you can understand the nuances of the DNA that drives you. Making the necessary changes to compensate for weaknesses such as the ones I've just identified are decisions you have to make.

Specialist DNA

A cross-quadrant DNA is always a good thing. If you are an Opportunist with Specialist DNA, that is a *very* good thing. Here's why.

Consider some of the Opportunist's *weaknesses*:

- Impulsive
- Unfocused
- Scattered and disorganized
- Performs in bursts of activity—like the hare in the story, "The Tortoise and the Hare"

Now consider some of the Specialist's *strengths*:

- Analytical
- Single-focused
- Methodical and organized
- Exhibits consistent activity over sustained periods of time— like the tortoise in the story, "The Tortoise and the Hare"

Pretty cool, huh? If you look at an Opportunist-Specialist, many of the Specialist's weaknesses are offset by the Opportunist's strengths. You can do the same by flipping this around.

You have an incredible opportunity to harness the best of both worlds, but it's going to take some work. It's rare to find an entrepreneur who has the perfect balance of Specialist DNA and Opportunist DNA. This means that most with this combination have a more dominant DNA. That dominant DNA will end up driving the majority of the decisions you make. I'm going to assume that Opportunist DNA is more dominant in you (because you are reading this section). If so, you need to actively tap into the Specialist DNA in you. If you are following the seven strategies I gave you, you'll end up engaging a coach. Make sure this is one of the areas your coach is holding you accountable for. A good coach will understand the nuances of your BOSI DNA so that he or she can help you balance decision making to leverage the best of both of your DNAs.

Innovator DNA

The right-quadrant combination of Opportunist-Innovator makes you a fun-loving, people-pleasing person who can't get a business to succeed if the whole world depended on it.

As an entrepreneur, you really have quite a few forces working against you. You already know the Opportunist forces that are working against you. Those weaknesses are further exaggerated with Innovator DNA.

Your Opportunist DNA thinks up great ideas and inventions and your Innovator DNA can develop the schematics and concepts. The problem is there is very limited business-building expertise available to speak of. You can try, but you'll be like the beagle trying to win a race against a bunch of steroid-filled greyhounds. It's going to be a pretty rough race.

But don't be dismayed, there is great news for you to rest on. You simply need to pick the right entrepreneurial venture and surround yourself with the right team.

Let's start with choosing the right entrepreneurial venture. Here's the thing. It can't be a business you are going to own and operate. Sorry. It just can't. You're not built to start up and *manage* a business. Instead, the right entrepreneurial venture for you will be one where you are partnered up with entrepreneurs who have left-quadrant DNA (Specialist and Builder). They should control a majority stake in the company, thereby assuming most of the risk and the operational headaches.

You, my friend, should then focus your energies on being out in the marketplace promoting your company's product or service. Use your people-friendly gifts as an Opportunist to travel the world as the face of the company. Get out of the operations side of the business and go earn a ton of frequent-flier miles.

You'll need some help staying organized and focused. Your coach will help you do that.

The Action Plan Checklist

Here is a quick action planner you can use to start the process of moving to deploy some of the strategies you have learned. You may choose to skip one or more strategies because you have intuitively optimized them already.

Strategy	Priority (1–7)	Start Date	Resources/People Needed
Optimize Your Business, Part 1: Build vs. Leverage			
Optimize Your Business, Part 2: Going "All In"			
Optimize Your Team, Part 1: Your Advisory Board			
Optimize Your Team, Part 2: Your Coach			
Optimize Your Credibility			
Optimize Your Work-Life Balance Plan			
Optimize Your Personal Leadership Development Plan			

Additional Tips

Here are a few more things to consider for your Opportunist DNA. Pick the appropriate DNA column that scored high on your BOSI Quiz.

	Builder
Business Model	You have the DNA to start up and build a company from the ground up. You are driven by exit strategy, so begin with the end in mind and prepare the company for sale from day one.
Lead Generation	You are well-suited for almost any form of lead generation including an in-house sales team.
Sales	Your company's follow-up systems will tend to be weak because you are too focused on landing the next big fish. Hire a consultant to find opportunity/profit leaks in your business. Doing so will make you millions.
Financing	Your best source of start-up and working capital is other Opportunists. Don't bother pursuing other BOSI DNAs. They won't invest in your company.
Human Resources	Hire administrative and office manager type of help. Outsource more creative work (Web development, SEO, social media, marketing) to credible firms.
Advisory Requirements	Lawyer, accountant, financial planner, and business coach

Specialist	Innovator
You are best suited to build up a small business, sell it, and start up another rather than being the person who builds a $50-million business over 20 years. Also consider leveraging a business opportunity rather than starting your own business.	Your DNA is not suited to start up and manage a business. The daily headaches of management and operations will drive you insane. Rather, outsource the functional parts of your business (production, fulfillment, finance) to capable firms.
Your best form of lead generation will come from building authority in your area of expertise (see the Specialist's seven strategies for more information).	Use dealers/distributors/affiliates for your primary form of lead generation and sales. Don't try to do your marketing or lead generation in-house.
The Opportunist in you will want to over-promise results. The Specialist in you will want to stick to facts and figures. Try to keep both DNAs in balance. You are better off hiring an outside sales person.	Let your dealers/distributors/affiliates figure out how to do the selling. You just need to focus on building and improving your product or service.
If you have a good credit rating and asset base, use debt financing. If not, use the same strategy as the Opportunist-Builder to the left.	Don't enter into debt financing. You are not built for structured payments/repayments. You will probably end up defaulting on your note and creating challenges.
Hire administrative and office manager type help. Outsource the more creative work (web development, SEO, social media, marketing) to credible firms. Strategy	Outsource as much as possible. Work from a comfortable home or a shared office facility.
Lawyer, accountant, financial planner, and business development expert	Lawyer, accountant, financial planner, and business coach

chapter

9

The Specialist DNA: "Three Cheers for the Tortoise"

Now we'll shift our attention to the Specialist DNA, the most popular Entrepreneurial DNA by a long shot. Our research shows that well over 50 percent of entrepreneurs have a Primary Specialist DNA. If I had to pick one word to describe the Specialist at the outset of this chapter, the word would be *expert*. Picking up on our story from Chapter 1, lets look at how a Specialist can take advantage of her particular entrepreneurial tendencies.

Overview
Sue Thomas is a certified public accountant (CPA) in Albany, New York. She is married to Jim. Combined, they make a comfortable six-figure income that provides a good lifestyle for them and their two children.

"I Did It for the Spread"
Sue went through what felt like countless hours of education, testing, and certification. She *earned* the letters CPA behind her name.

She started her career as an employee for a global accounting and tax firm. While there, she refined her skills, continued her education, gained some experience, and built a base of satisfied clients. Then one day, Sue looked at the spread between what her employer was charging for her time and what she was actually taking home.

"Wow!" she said. "That's a big spread."

"You should just start your own firm," Jim said.

She thought to herself, "I can keep more of the money, provide an even better, high-touch service, and be my own boss!"

After months and months of careful planning and consideration, Sue embarked on her entrepreneurial journey. Sue loves being her own boss. She loves the freedom and the control. She enjoys pulling into the parking lot of the Albany Business Park office complex to see her name on the door of suite 400. She smiles as she hears the receptionist, Laura, answer the phone, "Sue Thomas and Associates, how may I help you?"

"Ask Me for My Credentials"

I remember the feeling I had at age 17 when someone asked me if I was qualified to drive a car and I proudly displayed my driver's license to him. Sue feels the same way when people ask for her credentials. After all, she worked hard to earn the certification, degree, and letters after her name. As a matter of fact, those credentials are displayed proudly in walnut frames right in her office. Those credentials act as a form of credibility and validation for her. It helps her feel different than the typical small business owner who just slapped a Web site and brochure together and started selling "stuff" to people.

Along the way, Sue has also picked up some awards and recognition too. Those mementos share the wall and shelf space with her educational certificates. They are all there to tell a story to her prospects and clients: a story Sue would prefer for them to figure out by looking at the wall—so she doesn't have to appear like she is "pitching" herself. Sue is not the biggest fan of *selling*. That includes selling *herself* and being sold *to*. She doesn't sell;

she "generates referrals." She has kind of a "used car salesperson" view of most salespeople, and she certainly does not want to be perceived that way by her customer or client.

As a consequence, Sue often *undersells* herself. This is why Sue's credentials come in handy. If properly positioned in her office, the credentials can do the selling for her. And ideally, a referral will do the same thing. This is where networking comes in. Sue spends two or three nights a week at networking events. From fundraising events and chamber mixers to Parent-Teacher Association meetings and important parties, Sue uses these opportunities to network with people who can help her business grow. If you were to ask Sue her no. 1 source of new business, she would tell you it was referrals and networking.

Strangely enough, though, Sue found herself around a lot of competitors at networking events. So to separate herself from the crowd, she started to do some local speaking gigs. This way, she wasn't just "another face in the crowd," she was "the celebrity" in the room. Well, it didn't take long before every other CPA in town was doing speaking gigs at chamber of commerce events and meetups. How frustrating for Sue.

The Customer Is King

It didn't take long for Sue to figure out that if she just took excellent care of her customers, it would turn into referrals and repeat business. She didn't have to invest in complex follow-up systems and software. She just had to take better care of her clients than her competitors would.

She found that the better she got to know her customers the more loyal they became. There was Mr. Jones, the one with the golden retriever named Sam. Then there was Bill, the plumbing contractor whose daughter had just become an all-American at Purdue University. The list goes on and on of all the personal relationships Sue had built with her customers.

"My customers know that I care," she says. As a matter of fact, her office staff is actively engaged in similar customer service and relationship building too. A couple of the office assistants actually know more about some clients than even Sue does. And that is a good thing in Sue's book. However, Sue soon realized that *every one of her competitors was doing the exact same thing as she was!* In other words, all her competitors looked just like her, despite her belief that her firm was different. But the prospects just didn't see that. If only she could show those prospects her credentials, her satisfied clients, and her industry expertise. If only she could stand out in this very crowded marketplace.

This is the single-biggest frustration for a Specialist like Sue. The customer, the client, or the prospect finds it hard to differentiate one service provider from another.

Why? Because Sue and her other Specialist competitors are typically offering the same product or service *and* are all crowded together in the same *Yellow Pages*, coupon mailers, local print media, chamber promotions, and networking events. The good news for Sue is that there are strategies she can implement in her business to help her stand out and become the authority her prospects are looking for. It's going to require her to stretch her marketing muscles and step outside the box her competitors are marketing in, but the rewards for those actions will be nothing short of extraordinary.

"I Need More Traffic"

It bugs Sue that some entrepreneurs find lead generation so easy. It's almost like they were born to do it. Meanwhile, Sue is trying everything that comes naturally to her. Although her business is doing okay, it's not doing as well as it could. If she could just get more traffic of qualified prospects, things would be so much better. She tried hiring a marketing company to come up with some new ideas last year, but their ideas just didn't sit well with Sue.

She read the blogs of all the top marketing gurus. She attended the breakout session at her continuing education events. She took the notes. She asked the questions. She even came home and implemented some of the strategies, but they just didn't work as well as advertised. So she went back to what she always did—focusing on her expertise. If only she could get some more customer traffic through the front door.

"Set the Thermostat to 74 Degrees, Please"

Sue is not a big fan of risk. She isn't like those crazy entrepreneurs who jump without having calculated every possible scenario of the outcome. Omar Kelly is an off-and-on client of Sue's. Every time Omar tells her about his next outlandish business idea, she sighs (on the inside). "I'm nothing like him," she thinks. Sue is *not* easily distracted by glittering new business opportunities and money-making schemes like some of her clients. She is focused on her core business.

Sue is driven by the size of her personal income. Thinking back, as soon as her adjusted gross income reached her target range of $150,000, she was a happy camper. She had the nice home, the kids in private school, some nice toys of her own, a nice office. Sue was pretty comfortable. The internal entrepreneurial thermostat in Sue hit its ideal 74-degree temperature and the business *promoting* had stopped.

Despite being content, every once in a while Sue would look over the fence at a client, like Bob Morris, who was building a five- or ten-million-dollar-a-year company with lots of risk and growth. She wondered what it would be like to be bigger or grow her company *faster*. But the risks of having to change things, leverage money, bring in different staff, and do nontraditional marketing always brought her back to reality. Changing anything now would involve more risk and discomfort than Sue would bargain for.

Specialist DNA at Work

Specialists find it very easy to walk into their place of business and follow a methodical and systematic (often repetitive) set of tasks for the day. A significant majority of their time on the job is spent working *in* the business (as described by Michael Gerber in

The E-Myth). This means actually running the machinery, baking the dough, doing the surgery, delivering the consulting service, or clicking the keyboard and mouse. While other BOSI DNAs quickly get bored, distracted, and antsy in a structured and repetitive environment, Specialists don't.

Specialists deliver high-touch products and services to their customers. Customer loyalty is something Specialists covet and work hard to earn. They put a great deal of focus on customer satisfaction.

Specialists are gifted to build community together. They invest a disproportionate amount of time (relative to other BOSI DNAs), in community with each other. This includes networking events, continuing education programs, social mixers, and online communities. This is because Specialist DNA values professional relationships. Specialists understand that strong interpersonal professional relationships are the lifeblood to their businesses.

Specialist DNA at Home

Specialists find it much easier to switch out of work mode than those with other BOSI DNAs. It comes back to structure and focus—both strengths of this DNA. When Specialist DNA entrepreneurs get in the car to drive away from the office, they typically leave the office behind. Of course, there are exceptions to that rule, for example, when it is busy season or when a couple of last-minute files need some work at home. However, in general, work time is work time and home time is home time.

Because of this commitment to home time, Specialist DNA entrepreneurs lead a fairly balanced work-life routine. Dinner at home with the family is not the exception, it is typically the rule. Weekends off (unless a career requirement) are also quite the norm.

A Specialist can tend to be a bit overstructured in his or her home life. It is very hard for this type of entrepreneur to be around family members who don't appreciate order and a methodical approach to decision making. Most Specialist DNA entrepreneurs end up with spouses who demonstrate Opportunist DNA tendencies (opposites attract, after all). That makes for some interesting discussions on the home front, especially when one spouse wants to be very spontaneous and adventurous while the other wants a more controlled, predictable environment.

Specialist DNA at Its Best

Specialists are at their best when they perform the primary service that generates income for the business. The accountant crunches numbers, the doctor sees patients, and the developer writes code. This is what Specialist DNA entrepreneurs are bred to do and they do it very well. Specialists are also at their best when the business plan calls for steady, focused, methodical production and distribution of commoditized products and services. Food service, auto repair, home care, health care, financial management, grocery, and business services are just a few of those commoditized products and services.

As mentioned earlier in this chapter, Specialists are experts at building and maintaining community. They hand out and collect more business cards than any other BOSI DNA. Specialist DNA is also at its best in learning environments. Regardless of the Specialist's level of academic experience, he or she will dive deep and look to acquire as much professional development knowledge as possible.

Specialist DNA at Its Worst

Specialists are at their worst in two main areas. These are marketing and business development. The stronger one's Specialist DNA, the bigger the nightmare marketing becomes. There is much more on this topic in the next chapter. The second area where Specialists are at their worst is in asking for help. By nature, Specialists are quite self-reliant. That leads to an "I'll figure out how to do it myself" mind-set when dealing with uncharted territory like marketing. In some cases, it works to the entrepreneur's advantage. In most cases though, it takes the entrepreneur so far off course and eats up so much of his or her bandwidth, the activity often proves less fruitful than if it was given to someone else to do in the first place.

Ideal Business Ventures for Specialists

Specialists do extremely well in business ventures tied to their main line of education, past employment, or apprenticeship. When advising individuals with high Specialist DNA, I try to point them to something at which they are *already* proficient.

Entrepreneurs with low Specialist DNA make excellent candidates for ventures that have an established brand in place. Certain professional service/sales organizations and franchises such as State Farm Insurance, H&R Block, and ClosetMaid are examples of established brands in which Specialist DNA entrepreneurs really thrive. The bigger brand takes on the headaches of developing proven marketing systems. This allows the Specialist DNA entrepreneur to focus on providing the service and client relationship management.

Businesses for Specialists to Avoid

Specialist DNA is one of the most adaptive DNAs of all four BOSI DNAs. This means that, given enough time and the proper educational tools, this DNA can thrive in almost any business venture. With that said, there are some businesses that mid-to-high Specialist DNA should potentially steer clear of. Businesses that require a hard-selling approach rather than a consultative-selling approach, although lucrative, can leave the Specialist feeling like a fish out of water.

Another area to watch out for is the "make money fast" deals. It is not because Specialists cannot do well in those deals. It is because Opportunist DNA entrepreneurs tend to be quite active in those markets. Competing with Opportunists (natural-born promoters) in highly promotion-focused businesses can be frustrating for Specialists.

Some Tips on Partnerships and Alliances

One of the big mistakes Specialists tend to make is to align and collaborate almost exclusively with other Specialists. Although comfortable, this leads to very little innovation.

There are times when Specialist-Specialist collaboration works incredibly well. An organization like BNI International (www.bni.com) is a great example of a thriving venture whose membership is almost exclusively Specialists. The same is true for most lead sharing groups. I strongly encourage Specialist DNA entrepreneurs from noncompeting industries to work together, to share leads, and to advocate for each other's services.

A partnership or an alliance between two Specialists is a whole different animal. When two Specialists partner, the resulting business, although safe and stable, is typically unscalable and less valuable at the time of exit.

One way to create better and bigger results is to consider partnering with entrepreneurs in possession of different BOSI DNAs. Specialists represent a majority of small businesses in America and around the world. In order for Specialists to break past the small business space into mid-to-large company size almost always requires the involvement of partners with Builder DNA.

Specialist DNA Partnered with Builder DNA

Working with Builders in a business partnership can prove to be very profitable for Specialists. Builders tend to think globally and build highly scalable business models—things that don't come naturally to Specialists. In a partnership situation, the partner with Builder DNA can focus on strategic initiatives like business development, capital sourcing, and corporate strategy. Meanwhile, the partner with Specialist DNA can deploy his or her gifts in operational management, logistics, and service provision. The resulting business almost always has a higher growth rate and much higher exit value than one partnered with two Specialist DNAs.

Specialist DNA Partnered with Opportunist DNA

Opportunist DNA represents a cross-quadrant relationship to someone with Specialist DNA. This means the strengths of one DNA are typically the weaknesses of the other. In a partnership situation, this can be a very good thing. Opportunists tends to enjoy selling, marketing, and promotions. These are all things that Specialists would much rather not have to deal with. On the flip side, Specialists are excellent at getting routing tasks done, dealing with day-to-day operations, and managing people. These are all things that Opportunists would not be caught dead doing. Opportunist partners are also great at infusing a level of excitement and positive energy in a corporate environment—something lacking in Specialist-only companies.

Some Typical Statements Made by a Specialist

If you have ever made any of these statements, you have been exhibiting Specialist tendencies. Given your new knowledge about your Entrepreneurial DNA, think about these for a few minutes and see how they fit with your business.

- I started my business so I could be my own boss and earn a bigger income than a job could pay me.
- My no. 1 goal in business is to earn a healthy six-figure income from my business for 20+ years.

BOSI BUSINESS STRATEGY ALERT!

Don't rely on yourself or your industry peers to design your marketing strategy. Go outside your industry and find marketing systems that have worked. Then take those strategies and test them in your business. It sounds "risky" but doing so could prove to be quite rewarding.

- A big frustration is not being able to stand out from my competition, despite my credentials.
- I worked hard through schooling/apprenticeship/certification/how-to training to be in business today.
- I've been involved in the same industry for most of my corporate and entrepreneurial career.

- I am excellent at my primary trade, but I am not as good at selling and marketing.
- My primary education source is industry publications, journals, and events.
- Although hectic, I have a fairly fixed work schedule.
- I am not easily distracted, if ever, by other business opportunities or money-making deals.
- I am quite analytical when it comes to making decisions.
- I have a hard time asking for help or mentorship from people who do not have the same level of education or credentials as I have.
- My total tenure as owner of this company will exceed 15 years.
- I find it easy to hire and manage operational staff (administrative, finance, etc.). However, high-end sales and marketing people are a whole other story.
- I end up spending too much time working *in* my business rather than *on* my business.
- Referrals are my preferred source of new business.
- I use traditional advertising/marketing but rarely engage in high-risk or out-of-the-box marketing that other business owners use.
- My reputation in the community is a very important part of my brand and business success.

BOSI BUSINESS STRATEGY ALERT!

The routine of business has its way of stumping passion and excitement in life. What can you do in the next 90 days to shake things up a bit? What is that one *big* risk you have always wanted to take that could set you on a whole new course of achievement?

- I'd rather borrow and repay money than have equity partners.
- Networking is a big part of my long-term marketing plan.

- My competitors promote virtually the same product/service I do. The main way I differentiate myself is through high-touch service.
- Cold prospecting/calling is not part of my marketing plan.
- We are active members of our chamber and other networking groups.
- I don't consider myself a "big dreamer." I am more conservative and methodical in my business growth plan.
- Friends and family always come to me for free advice in my area of expertise.
- I'd rather be the slow and steady tortoise in the race than the fast moving, risk-taking hare.

The Specialist DNA at a Glance

STRENGTHS	WEAKNESSES	FRUSTRATIONS
Specialists study to excel at their trade and invest in continuing education. This gives them an advantage over some other Entrepreneurial DNA types.	The Specialist gets stuck in the box when it comes to growth strategy. That may prevent the venture from achieving its true potential.	It is hard for a Specialist to stand out in a crowded marketplace of competitors who appear to offer the same product/ service.
Being relatively risk-averse keeps Specialists from taking unnecessary risks when unrelated business opportunity knocks at the door.	It is hard for Specialists to transition from an *hourly rate* mind-set to a *leveraged distribution* mind-set. This means having to staff *up* for the company to grow.	Specialists get frustrated watching other Specialist competitors use price drops as a way to get prospects in the door.
Specialists recognize the importance of personal relationships in business and put emphasis on building healthy relationships with clients and employees.	Specialists tend not to go outside their industry for expertise and advice. This strategy, although safe, prevents them from accessing "game changing" strategies.	Specialists get frustrated by their inability to keep high-output administrative staff from leaving and manage the revolving door of human resources.

10

Seven Business Optimization Strategies for Specialist DNA

Specialist DNA positions you for a steady, predictable business journey. You are pre-equipped with a set of outstanding gifts and strengths. We learned about those unique strengths in the previous chapter. But we also learned about some compelling weaknesses. This chapter is designed to give you some *actionable strategy* on how to leverage your innate strengths while compensating for your potential weaknesses. Think of it as an optimization process. In some cases, we will be fixing something that is broken. In other cases, we will be taking proactive and precautionary strategies. In a couple of areas, we may not have to do a thing! You may have intuitively taken the necessary optimization steps already.

Showing up every morning to a business that isn't optimized for your Entrepreneurial DNA can be a very frustrating thing. As long as you find yourself competing in the weeds without a unique selling proposition (USP), you will be swimming upstream. The seven strategies we will be discussing in this chapter are designed to make sure you get to your long-term vision while enjoying the journey getting there. The seven strategies we'll discuss are:

- Optimize Your Strategic Plan
- Optimize Your Business Development
- Optimize Your Advisory Team
- Optimize Your Mastermind Team
- Optimize Your Expert Status
- Optimize Your Work-Life Balance Plan
- Optimize Your Exit Strategy and Potential

Strategy One: Optimize Your Strategic Plan

For this section, I want to tap into your vision. Here's my first question for you:

> "Given where you are in your business journey today, where do you see the maximum potential for your company's size and value? Is the maximum potential already achieved, or is the potential 2 times or 20 times bigger than today?"

Based on that answer, here's the next question:

> "Are you energized to take the company to that maximum potential or have you hit a comfort zone or obstacle?"

The reason I want you to percolate on the above questions is so you can get to a point where you can decide what comes next.

> "Is the next step in your business journey to hold, grow, or exit? What is the next logical step in your entrepreneurial journey, and are you ready for it?"

If you know the answers to the above questions, it is time to take a good hard look at the strengths and weaknesses of your

Entrepreneurial DNA and figure out how to leverage them to make the outcome you want a reality.

If *growth and expansion* is the next step in the vision, chances are your Entrepreneurial DNA will kick in and find 50 reasons why now is *not* the time to grow. After all, there's the economy, political unrest, daily business fires, and homeless puppies in the way. Right? That's the Specialist DNA at work.

To overcome this obstacle, go back to your vision and dream for the company you started. Remind yourself why you even went into business—to provide a better quality of life for your family, or to capitalize on your hard-earned skills. Then, resolve to either stay the course or chart a new path.

If the decision is to chart a fresh new path, get on with it and get it done. Don't let the analytical risk-averse Specialist in you slow things down more than is absolutely necessary. Take the time this year to get away from your office for a day or two and spend time building a three-year strategic plan. A good strategic plan answers two main questions:

1. Where are you going? (Your vision.)
2. How are you going to get there? (Your mission.)

Use the series of exercises I have provided you in Part Three of this book. I can assure you that your business will be the better for it.

Strategy Two: Optimize Your Business Development

If you are like most Specialists, you have an incredible talent for providing your product or service to your customers. But truth be told, you are frustrated with the business development side of your business. Even if you are proficient at generating new business, the problem is that new business development is 100 percent dependent on you! Every time you take the focus off business development to do something else in your business, the train tends to slow down. You wish you could just pay someone to do it well, but there is a struggle within you to keep your brand from appearing like the stereotype of a "used-car lot."

You probably recognize that there are some things that you are really good at doing. Then there are things that you just enjoy doing. Here's my question for you: Is business development something *you enjoy doing*? If the answer is yes, and you feel like you are succeeding with it, then you can skip this part of the strategy and go to the next one. Otherwise, read on.

If business development is something *you do because you have to*, not because you love to, then consider outsourcing your business development to someone who loves doing it. Remember the analogy of the pit bull, the retriever, and the greyhound? Specialists are like greyhounds to me. You are highly talented in a core area of your business. But nobody can be good at everything, right? So unless you are a greyhound in business development, you are working *outside* your giftedness. That means others who do enjoy business development will outperform you in the marketplace. They will be working *within* their giftedness.

The purpose of this book is to have you take a good inventory of your strengths, talents, and gifts, and then hand everything else off to people who are just as strong, talented, and gifted in those other areas. Doesn't that make good common sense?

"But it is going to cost a lot of money hiring all those people and experts," you say.

"Not necessarily," is my answer to you. It only costs money if it doesn't generate a reasonable ROI I've been in the boat where I paid "experts" to build my Web site, drive online traffic, generate leads, and the list goes on. So believe me when I say, I understand the hesitation to outsource. However, if you deal with highly credible firms that have expertise in certain niches, you can save a tremendous amount of money in overhead costs while getting a significant ROI. Let me give you an example.

For the longest time, one of my companies did our Internet marketing in-house. I hired a guy who promised me the stars.

I paid him a healthy monthly retainer to do nothing but build traffic for us and our clients. Months and quarters went by and we were no further along than we were when we first started. See, I hired someone who said he could do it rather than someone who had a proven track record. I hired locally (and through friends) because I thought that was the right thing to do.

Does that sound uncomfortably familiar? Shopping local and hiring friends is just fine, but I have resolved to shop locally for produce not expertise. In this competitive marketplace, I have to shop nationally (and sometimes globally) for the best solutions for my company. I'd encourage you to do the same.

So I went on a national search. After months of homework and vetting, I found an search engine optimization (SEO) firm and a social media firm that were getting A+ verified results. I handed them the keys to the car and told them to drive. Was it scary to do that? Of course it was. But when I took the plunge, here's what I found. My costs went down, my ROI went through the roof, and I gained some incredible business alliances as a result of it. (As a side note, the SEO firm ended up being in the same city I'm in. But I did a national search and picked the best. It just happened to be that the firm was in my own backyard).

Start with strategy. Bring in a sought-after marketing strategist firm (not the one-man show in your chamber of commerce). Pay them for their time to build an out-of-the-box, scalable marketing plan with and for you. Be aware that given your Specialist DNA, you will be drawn to hire someone with Specialist DNA. That is not an optimum choice. You are better off engaging someone with Primary Builder DNA or Primary Innovator DNA to help you build your marketing strategy. Once the strategy is built, you can have an individual or firm with Specialist DNA do the execution for you.

There are amazing firms who can do it better and faster than anyone you could employ. Let those firms do the employing for you. We'll do our best to keep a vetted list of such firms on the BOSI Web site.

In Appendix A, I have included the SPACE funnel I use when building marketing strategy with entrepreneurs. Use it as a tool to begin the internal discussion on how you can find Suspects—those potential clients before they are solid Prospects—and move them to Prospects and eventually to Accounts, Clients, and Evangelists. Question what systems you have put in place at every step of the process to ensure that people keep moving through the funnel, rather than getting stuck or lost. If you hit some roadblocks in the strategic process—engage an expert. Sound strategy is one of the best places you can invest your money.

I have seen a lot of Specialists transform their companies by outsourcing certain business development functions like creative direction, Internet marketing, sales training, and marketing strategy. If you take an honest inventory of your in-house staff's capabilities, you may find yourself making the same decision. Take the step of outsourcing alone, and your business will grow faster and you'll be able to focus your time and energies on what you really love to do.

Strategy Three: Optimize Your Advisory Team

The Specialist DNA in you makes you an excellent advisor. You have expertise—expertise that others seek. But there is a flip side to this situation. The Specialist DNA in you tends not to trust or hire other experts. Maybe it is the analytical side of you. Maybe there is a bit of pride involved in asking for help. Regardless, in many cases, the reality ends up being that the Specialist ends up going it alone.

Sure, the Specialist will network. But that's not the same as having advisors.

So I'd like to encourage you to step beyond the traditional attorney and accountant relationships and add some other experts to your paid advisory team. One such expert may be a business coach who can keep you accountable for executing parts of your strategy in which you tend to slow down. Another expert may be a sales/marketing advisor who can help you build and execute growth strategy. Don't be shy asking for help and certainly don't pinch pennies trying to do it in-house.

My guess is that you have a high-value product and/or service at your company. My guess is also that not enough people know about that amazing product and/or service. Let's change that. One step in that direction is to expand your advisory team to include experts who can help you get past the obstacles that your Specialist DNA puts in the way of growth and strategy.

Strategy Four: Optimize Your Mastermind Team

Specialists enjoy masterminding with other entrepreneurs. It is a great way to share ideas, learn, and even engage in some good old-fashioned networking and referral generation.

Masterminding is a great tool in any entrepreneur's toolbox. I just want to make sure you tweak your mastermind team (if necessary) to make sure you're not sitting around a bunch of clones of yourself. That is not going to do anyone any good.

In other words, a CPA masterminding with other CPAs, lawyers, graphic designers, and restaurant owners is great for building relationships, but not optimal for business development. You are all virtually the same BOSI Profile.

In a best-case scenario, you'll have a couple of Builder DNA Profiles in your mastermind team. They'll encourage you to scale up, expand, and spend more time building your business rather than working on the small details. That is a message a Specialist needs to hear over and over again.

But let me tell you the best BOSI Profile for you to mastermind with. It's the Opportunist BOSI Profile. Since Opportunists are cross-quadrant from you, you can bet that they are totally and completely opposite of you. They are probably involved in multilevel marketing (MLM), real estate speculation, offshore trading, and a dozen other money-making ventures. You probably look at entrepreneurs like them and shake your head in disdain. Little did you know that they could become your most powerful business allies.

Those with Opportunist Entrepreneurial DNA may appear
to be complete lunatics to you. But they complement your Entrepreneurial DNA because your biggest weaknesses are their greatest strengths.

• You tend to hate "promoting." They love it.
• You tend to think the sky is falling. They think today is the
  greatest day to be alive (even if the bank is repossessing most
  of their earthly goods).
• You are the tortoise. They are hares.

The two of you make a great team!

So take a look at the people you mastermind with. Make sure
you have some diversity of BOSI Profiles represented in your group.

Don't look at your differences as barriers but as learning
opportunities and you'll see your business improve. If you don't
have a mastermind team in which you are an active and regular
participant, I'd like to encourage you to get that organized immediately. Check out CEO organizations like Vistage (http://www.
Vistage.com), where you can plug into an existing infrastructure
of groups, chairs, and national support. If your resources allow, I
would certainly recommend Vistage. I have enjoyed the benefit of
that organization myself and recommend it strongly.

You have also probably heard of BNI International (http://
www.bni.com) or are already a member. BNI is an excellent
networking and lead generation opportunity. Just make sure that
your local BNI group has a good blend of Entrepreneurial DNAs.
Talk to your group leader if you notice an overabundance of Specialist DNAs in the room. The group will need to try to balance
out those DNAs so you and your peers can get the best value for
your investment of time and resources.

If cash is tight, there are networking groups that organize
through the BOSI site, Meetup (http://www.meetup.com), and
LinkedIn Groups. Just understand that there is a massive difference
between networking and masterminding. Networking events are

great places to keep your business card printer in business. How-ever, you also need to be part of a small group of trusted peers who will hold you accountable in business.

Strategy Five: Optimize Your Expert Status

One of the most important strategies I want to share with you is the importance of your building expert status in the marketplace. Now I know I am preaching to the choir. This is something you have been working on since the day you opened the doors of your business. But I just want to give you my two cents worth on some ways to take this strategy to the next level.

Here's why. Your Entrepreneurial DNA thrives on being perceived as an expert in your field. Interestingly enough, your customers appreciate that too. You have a copy of the SPACE funnel in Appendix A, but I've brought it here (see Figure 10-1) to show you how important this strategy is for you.

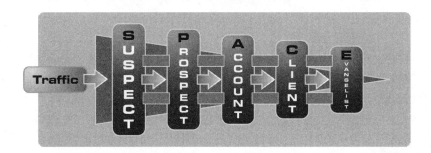

Figure 10-1 The SPACE™ Marketing Funnel

This is your marketing funnel. The first step in the marketing journey is to identify your "Suspects," also known as your target audience. If I were to ask you the question, "Who is the person *and* what is the situation for which your company is *always* the best choice?" The answer to that question would be your target audience—your Suspects.

You can learn more about this in the Appendix and on the BOSI Web site, but here's the deal. Your Suspects will not become

"Prospects" (people who raise a hand and become leads), until they have a level of trust in your expertise. I don't care if you sell pizza, accounting services, dog food, or auto body repair. Your Suspects must see you as a credible market leader in order for them to pick up the phone, fill out a Web form, or walk into your lobby. Keep in mind that a Suspect's definition of "market leader" differs based on who he or she is and what he or she is shopping for. Sometimes, just the fact that you know more than the Suspect does on a given topic makes you the "expert the Suspect is looking for."

So knowing that the Suspect wants you to be the expert he or she is looking for, the question then becomes, *how can you be perceived as that expert*? I use the word "perceived" because this really is a case of "perception is reality."

If a Suspect goes on to Google or Yahoo! and searches for "Wichita Pizza," "Fort Worth Accountant," or "auto body repair," the search engine is going to act as an expert locator and display the results *it* feels are the most relevant.

I'm not pitching you on search engine optimization (SEO) services. I'm helping you get inside the head of your Suspects to understand what they are looking for.

The days of placing ads and mailing people blanket offers to generate leads are gone. Today, Suspects are reading online reviews, customer ratings, and they trust their social networks.

This is why you need to get the story of your company's expertise out into the digital ecosystem. You have to populate the digital ecosystem (social media, Web sites, search engines, video portals, etc.) with content about you and your company. I'm not talking about "who we are and why we're so great" content. I'm talking about education and information that will help your Suspects connect with you and recognize your expertise. I'm also talking about engaging your Clients and Evangelists to advocate for your expertise within their social networks.

If I was going to interview you on a topic you are truly the expert on, what would that topic be? Stop right now and think about that. You may be able to make a list of five to ten topics. Make that list in the box below.

Topics I'm an Expert On

For example: Quick tasty meals you can cook at home.

(This is a great topic for restaurant owners to share.)

1. _____

2. _____

3. _____

4. _____

5. _____

Now that you have your areas of expertise, make a list of all the ways you can get this content out to the marketplace. I'll start with a few suggestions.

- Your blog and microblogs
- Short videos on video portals (like YouTube and Vimeo, a video-sharing Web site)
- Local seminars/workshops (Think in terms of a restaurant showing people how to make their own sushi or a CPA showing people how to do their own taxes.)
- Local radio or TV talk/news shows (The media is hungry for good content.)

- Articles in periodicals
- Guest posts on high-traffic blogs (They are hungry for content too.)

Find other ways to get your expertise out into the marketplace in a big way. You'll find more Suspects knocking on your door, ready to become Prospects.

Then comes the really scary part. Having to sell them on becoming an Account! But that's a whole other seminar. Right? Or, your Opportunist business partner can take this role.

The bottom line is this. You must put a specific and actionable game plan in place to get your expertise out in the marketplace. Ask your mastermind team to keep you accountable to make sure you are staying consistent on pushing relevant, expertise-highlighting content out into the marketplace.

Strategy Six: Optimize Your Work-Life Balance Plan

You schedule staff meetings, client appointments, supplier conference calls, and shareholder meetings. Once those items are on your calendar, they get done, right?

Well, you need to develop a comprehensive work-life balance plan that schedules in time for rest, relaxation, family, and spirituality. Without it, you won't have a fulfilling business journey. You'll look up one day, and you'll be 20 years older and the best years of your life will be behind you.

Get out there and have some FUN. A good friend of mine who is a financial planner really has this down pat. Two to three times a month, I get Facebook updates suggesting that he is skiing somewhere, on a road trip, or spending an extra day after a business meeting in Phoenix just to take in the sights. Are you doing that? Are you enjoying your entrepreneurial journey? Or are you like most Specialists who plan and execute the annual family vacation with the same regimented order that they do a staff meeting or client presentation?

Do the same with your health. Find some FUN ways to improve your health. Your DNA tends to look for methodical systems to follow. That's good. But every once in a while, shake things up. If you need help with that, get together with the Opportunists in your mastermind team. They'll have plenty of wild plans for you to participate in.

Also, start to schedule regular time away from the office. Start with working from home one day per month. Then raise that to one day per week. Take one weekend a quarter away with your spouse. Without exception, take one month a year away from your business. That may sound impossible at this moment as you read this book, but I can virtually guarantee that it will force you to build a more scalable and sellable business.

Strategy Seven: Optimize Your Exit Strategy and Potential

I know your business is sellable. Don't get me wrong. But what's wrong with making it *more sellable*?

By *more sellable* I mean making it more desirable to the buyer. To investigate this further, let's put ourselves in the mind of the buyer. What would you and I want if we were buying a business?

- A stable revenue stream
- A consistent and replenishing source of leads/new business
- A plug-and-play operation (so the buyer can step in and take it over)
- A brand that isn't going to lose value when the seller leaves
- An operation that allows the buyer to still have a good quality of life

How is your business doing with this buyer checklist? There's room for improvement right? So start working toward that end. Let's pick two of the items and dive a bit deeper into how to position the company for a greater exit value.

A Consistent and Replenishing Source of Leads/New Business

The first thing that comes to mind here is organic traffic from the search engines and social media networks. Think of your Web site as a piece of real estate. If nobody can find your real estate (because it is swampland in Louisiana), then it has lower value than if, say, your property was in Times Square, New York. In Strategy Five, we talked about building authority or expertise. If you do that over the next two to three years and gain a healthy position of authority with the search engines, you'll have an asset that someone will gladly pay a premium for.

My friend Bob just sold his piece of "real estate" for $16,000,000 (yes, I double-checked the zeros). He still has his company, his customers, computers, employees, and revenues. He just sold his Web site, changed the name of his company, and continued on. That's the power and value of a consistent and replenishing source of leads/new business.

A Brand That Isn't Going to Lose Value When the Seller Leaves

Specialist companies are notorious for being undervalued at the time of sale because of the expected "attrition" when the former owner steps aside. The assumption is that when the owner leaves, some customers will stop shopping there. That's NUTS! Don't let that happen to your company after you have sunk your blood, sweat, time, and tears into it for so long. Build your business model so it is *not* dependent on you. I know that sounds crazy when you are an accountant, a chef, a doctor, or an electrician. But there is a way.

Certainly, there is a window of time in any business when you fit the idiom of being *chief, cook, and bottle washer*. But if you don't watch out, you'll be wearing all those hats 15 years from now. The entire business will be dependent on you. Every client relationship will rest on your shoulders. Every problem will require your attention.

Take the time now to look at your business model to figure out how to make your business more sellable. If the solution doesn't come easily to you, this may be one of those times to execute Strategy Three and find an expert who can help you get that done. I can assure you the few thousand dollars you'll spend on that expert will come back a hundredfold when you're sitting across from your buyer at the negotiating table.

A company that runs on its own brand position, rather than the owner/operator's name and fame, is significantly more valuable in a purchase transaction. I want to make sure that your company is selling for a multiple of 4 times to 10 times, rather than a fraction to 100 percent of current revenues.

Final Words about the Seven Strategies

So there we have it—seven areas where you can dive in and optimize your company (and life) based on who you are built to be. Pay extra-close attention to Strategies Two, Five, and Seven. That is where you will see the most significant return on investment (ROI) for your time, attention, and resources.

Factoring In Your Secondary DNAs

Chances are you have a Builder, Opportunist, or Innovator Secondary DNA. You may even have a combination of two or even three of them as your Secondary DNA. With that in mind, focus on the DNA that you scored the second-highest number of points on in the BOSI Test and follow the suggestions provided for that DNA combination.

Builder DNA

If you have Secondary Builder DNA, then chances are you have built a larger business (in size and scope) than your typical Specialist competitors. If the typical Specialist in your market builds a company with revenues of $400,000 per year, chances are your company does two to three times that revenue or more.

You have the DNA to build a thriving single-location or multi-location business enterprise. The Builder DNA in you will want to stretch out to multiple locations or some other leveraged distribution model. If you do pursue expansion of any nature, make sure to build systems and empower your managers with true authority. The Specialist in you will want to micromanage everything at every location. Use the Builder DNA in you to create systems and layers of empowered management, and then get out of the way. Don't get stuck in your business as a manager or service provider, especially in an expanding multi-location business. You'll kill yourself, and your family, along the way.

When it comes to lead generation, your growth rate will demand a steady and predictable source of leads. Online marketing/digital marketing will be a huge part of your brand's future growth. Focus on it, and invest in it now.

Given that you have a Specialist-Builder DNA combination, you are a left quadrant entrepreneur. One of the killer weaknesses of being a left quadrant entrepreneur is how stoic and flat-out *mean* you can appear to be around your staff. Unless you have found the grace to change that in your modus operandi, your sales team will have morale issues. Beyond focusing on making the personal improvement yourself, make sure to invest in personal development and outside training to keep your troops fired up. It will be a necessary piece to keep them performing to your extremely high demands.

When it is time to finance the start-up or growth of your venture, you are an excellent candidate for debt financing. Equity financing is an option, but handle that decision with care. If you have mastered your tendency to be prideful and egotistical already, then pursue equity financing and expect lots of "input" from your investment partners. However, if pride and ego are growth areas for you at this time, don't add fuel to the fire by bringing partners into the mix. Stay with debt financing or consider bringing in silent investors.

Your human resources (HR) strategy doesn't have to change much with a Specialist-Builder DNA. Hire administrative and management team members within your company. However, outsource the more creative work (Web development, search engine optimization (SEO), social media, marketing) to credible third-party firms. The Builder DNA in you will want to hire all those creative positions and control them in-house. The problem is that at the rate at which technology and skill are changing today, your in-house staff will never be able to keep up with a third-party firm that specializes in that task. Also, the Builder DNA in you could have some Jekyll and Hyde experiences in the office environment. Keeping your in-house staff small limits any potential exposure.

Chances are, your advisory team is missing a business development advisor. Consider adding one to the mix of your business. I know it's hard to admit you don't have the business development piece under control, but I am confident you will see some breakthrough results by engaging that expert on your team.

Plan to Be Thrown Off the Island

Depending on where you are in your entrepreneurial journey, you may be reading this a bit late in the game. I mentioned this point at the beginning of this section, but it is worth repeating. Your Builder DNA will allow you to do things your Specialist peers will not like. You'll break many of the rules of marketing that other Specialists have. They won't like that, and they will possibly ostracize you from their inner circle. If you have an SB (Specialist Builder) Profile, you have probably already experienced this in some way, shape or form.

Opportunist DNA

The Specialist-Opportunist (SO) Profile is one of the most popular BOSI DNA combinations. It makes for a fairly well-balanced entrepreneur, on the outside. The reason I say "on the outside" is because the Specialist-Opportunist entrepreneur is kind of like a duck in a pond—calm and collected *above* the water but paddling like crazy *under* the water. A lot of the paddling takes place in this type of entrepreneur's head. That's because the angel-and-devil-on-your-shoulder thing is really pronounced with this DNA combination. Specialist-Opportunist is a cross-quadrant DNA, which means that the things one DNA loves to do are the exact things the other DNA despises to do.

For example, the Specialist in you is highly skilled at a core task. Left to its own resources, the Specialist DNA would have a steady, methodical, and well-organized business and life. But that assumes the Specialist DNA is actually left to its own resources. The Opportunist would have nothing boring like that taking place. So it proceeds to bring disorganization, procrastination, and impulsiveness to the table just to shake things up. Don't get me wrong, the Specialist-Opportunist DNA combination is a great one. However, being aware of the nuances of each DNA will allow you to recognize when one DNA is generating some not-so-good results.

When it comes to your business model, the Opportunist in you will not be satisfied with a methodical and cookie-cutter core business. If you have a relatively small amount of Opportunist DNA in you, then focus on the Specialist game plan and watch for the Opportunist to pop up when you're making big decisions.

However, if you have a good amount of Opportunist DNA in you, consider stretching your Opportunist muscle by engaging in a part-time business opportunity on the side (investing, multilevel marketing, real estate, etc.). This will keep your Opportunist tendencies happy while staying out of the day-to-day operation of your core business.

Here's a word of caution when it comes to sales. Sales is one of the areas where your yin-and-yang DNAs will drive you nuts. The Specialist in you will try to overcomplicate the sales process by giving Prospects too much information with facts and figures. You will also be petrified to ask for the sale—because that will make you look like a dreaded "salesperson." Meanwhile, the Opportunist in you will tend to oversell or overstate the deliverables of your product/service. If you have an Specialist-Opportunist DNA Profile, you probably know exactly what I'm talking about right now. It must be the most frustrating thing on earth to have to sell and negotiate with people. It is just such a nightmare of an experience. As a solution, consider engaging an outside salesperson to do the selling for you.

When financing your business, stick with debt financing. However, make sure the business plan or repayment plan you have built was not driven by the blue-sky Opportunist in you. Double-check the numbers, be realistic, and trust the Specialist in you so that you set reasonable expectations for your lender/investor.

As far as human resources (HR) strategy goes, outsource as many job functions as you can beyond administrative support in your office. I'm talking about sales, digital marketing, graphic design, and IT-type services. You'll have less stress in your life as a result of it. Remember the picture of the duck on a pond. Even though you may look like you are a great manager to everyone around you, all that paddling will probably suck the life right out of you. Outsource as much as possible for your own sanity. As a side effect, all your outsource vendors could become great lead sources for your business.

I've got one more recommendation given your Opportunist DNA. Consider hiring a performance coach or business advisor to spend an hour or two each month with you to set and achieve goals. The Opportunist in you will come up with so many great ideas. The Specialist in you will have the technical ability to make those ideas a reality. However, if left uncontrolled, very little will get accomplished. In the bigger picture, the frustration factor (and sleepless nights) will simply escalate. A coach who understands your Entrepreneurial DNA, and how to work with it, will be able to help you get the most out of your amazing yin-and-yang DNA combination.

Remember, the Specialist is the tortoise and the Opportunist is the hare. Your Specialist-Opportunist Profile means you are *both*. So let the Specialist in you build methodology and consistency, but let the Opportunist in you spread its wings and bring some excitement and good old-fashioned risk to the table.

Innovator DNA

Secondary Innovator DNA means you are a lower-quadrant entrepreneur. Business development, marketing, and selling will be major stumbling blocks if you have a Specialist-Innovator DNA. You can do all of these tasks, but they will not come easy.

Your business model should focus on generating scalable revenues from the sale of your product/service rather than selling your time. For example, if you are an educator of sorts, avoid making your full living on live speaking events. As lucrative as that can be, you'll go crazy traveling and living out of a suitcase. More importantly, you'll max out your income-earning potential pretty quickly.

Instead, look to distribute your knowledge in formats that are easier to leverage. Blog more. Write and sell e-books. Record coursework and sell it on your Web site. Get a publisher to take on your book idea. The point is that your Specialist-Innovator Profile tells me that you are a *subject matter expert*. You are really good at what you do. Leverage that expertise so that an hour of your work generates tenfold to a hundredfold of a return rather than just a one-time return.

When it comes to marketing yourself, it's all about getting your expert status out to the marketplace. Hire a pay-for-placement public relations (PR) agent and let the world hear about your expertise. If your PR agent does his or her job well, you'll have appearances booked with local and national media. You'll probably also get invited to contribute articles to periodicals, inside and outside your industry. Those in turn will lead to more business opportunity. Have a credible digital marketing company advise you on how to maximize your online footprint. Get some press releases out into the marketplace about your latest breakthroughs and use that as a means to fuel more traffic to your product or service.

However, I'll say it again—make sure you have a business model that doesn't require you to trade time for dollars. Modify your business model to scale up without you. If you need help, visit the BOSI community online and find some vetted experts who can help you with your business model.

I'd strongly recommend using outside salespeople, dealers, or distributors to do your selling for you. It will be too hard for you to switch from expert to salesperson, at the drop of a hat, every time a business opportunity comes your way. If you have an online product, set up and promote your affiliate program. Let your dealers/distributors/affiliates figure out how to do the selling. You should just focus on building and delivering your product or service.

When it comes to financing your company, you are best-suited for friends-and-family capital sourcing since you carry a lot of credibility with that audience. If you do find a business partner who has a Builder-Opportunist Profile, you may have a very powerful business partnership opportunity. Make sure he or she invests in the business partnership; don't just hand him or her the car keys without skin in the game. Venture capital (VC) funding and Angel funding may elude you since venture capitalists tend to look for the Builder DNA when investing in entrepreneurial ventures. Debt financing is always an option, but could be a source of unnecessary burden on you and your company.

As a lower-quadrant entrepreneur, you love and work very well with people (including staff). You'll have a very happy and loyal staff, so hire away. Just keep the business development/marketing work outsourced. Since business development and marketing are weaknesses for your DNA, hiring someone (who reports to you) to do the job is the equivalent of an arsonist marrying a fire dancer. It is just not the best combination on earth. There are great full-service marketing companies that can sit down with you, map out a marketing plan, and handle the full execution so you don't have to.

Summary

If you are a mutt, like most entrepreneurs, focus on your Primary DNA. Also pay close attention to the modified strategy I've given you to compensate for your Secondary DNA. Being aware is 90 percent of the battle. Hopefully as early as this week, you'll find yourself thinking, "Gosh, that must be the Builder in me talking!" In most cases, you'll just laugh off your Secondary DNAs. But in some cases, you'll make a tactical move to compensate for a weakness in your Primary DNA or a strength of your Secondary DNA.

The Action Plan Checklist

Here is a quick action planner you can use to start the process of moving to deploy some of the strategies you have learned. You may choose to skip one or more strategies because you have intuitively optimized them already.

Optimization Points	Priority (1-7)	Start Date	Resources/People Needed
Optimize Your Strategic Plan			
Optimize Your Business Development			
Optimize Your Advisory Team			
Optimize Your Mastermind Team			
Optimize Your Expert Status			
Optimize Your Work-Life Balance Plan			
Optimize Your Exit Strategy and Potential			

11

The Innovator DNA: "Fish Out of Water"

Last but certainly not the least in our group of BOSI DNAs is the Innovator. This particular entrepreneur is characterized by one word—breakthrough. Innovators are the mad scientists of our world. They apply their mad scientist gifting in kitchens, garages, studios, and labs around the world. Returning to our story from Chapter 1, I'll show you how that Innovator can best run her business, given her entrepreneurial tendencies.

Overview

Ingrid Fuller is a health scientist who really didn't plan on being a business owner. She went into health sciences to find a cure for her daughter's debilitating illness. Two PhDs later, she found the solution, and it saved her daughter's life. Then the phone began to ring from people who wanted to get their hands on her product. Within 2 years, there were over 600 doctors ordering and stocking her product in their offices. Ingrid was overwhelmed by running a business. She just wanted to save her daughter's life and help other people.

"It Just Kind of Happened"

When I asked Ingrid the question, "Why did you start your business?" I got a response similar to that of others with Innovator DNA. She said, "I didn't really mean to start a business. I was doing something I really loved doing, and the business just kind of grew up around me."

For the Innovator, like Ingrid, you didn't begin your work with the plan of starting a business or making money. All you started with was an idea, which you turned into a product or service, and then you discovered that people wanted that product or service. People literally came to you and said, "How can I buy some of this from you? This is incredible. You should start a business."

I have had the fortune of working with a handful of them along the way. It is interesting for me to see a pattern in which their innovation typically comes from some sort of emotional life experience. It's not the case all the time, but it is more often than not.

It was an emotional trigger that got Ingrid started. Her daughter was the one who was sick. However, the doctors could not diagnose the problem. Her young child's health kept deteriorating to the point of imminent death. This loving mother determined that, "If no one can tell me how to help my baby, I'm going to figure it out myself!"

In the process of her search, Ingrid ended up getting two PhDs. Over the course of almost eight years, she found what she believed was the answer, and developed her product line. It saved her daughter's life. The journey helped her discover her personal mission. She was going to use her discovery to change the world. She shared it with people in need, and it worked, and the orders kept coming in.

The Weight of the World

Ingrid is driven by the desire to change the world, even if it is one person at a time. She loves the feeling she gets when she sees her product impact the quality of a person's life. When she hears, "I am feeling better!" or "Your product has changed my daughter," or "My quality of life has improved!" she is beside herself with tears of joy. Conversely, though, if a client is having a bad day, *she's* having a bad day. If 10 clients are having a bad day, *she's* having a horrible day. As with anything else, there is a good and bad side to this. Ingrid can easily get overloaded. If she is dealing with clients in a face-to-face setting, she can get overwhelmed as she finds herself carrying her client's burdens and stress. Ingrid Fuller, as an Innovator, is the complete opposite of Bob Morris, the Builder. Bob has an iron-clad firewall between business and personal life. Ingrid, however, can't see how someone's personal life is not totally and completely connected to how he or she acts in business.

Because of this, Ingrid has a very different perception about business than our other Entrepreneurial DNA types. Bob Morris, Sue Thomas, and Omar Kelly went into business for very specific reasons, but they *intentionally* entered the business world. Ingrid did not. And even once she got in, she started to perceive the business world as a selfish, "every person for him- or herself" type of world. She saw the profit motive, the greed, the manipulation, and the actions of big businesses and small suppliers. It certainly did not motivate her to want to be like them.

Ingrid really doesn't "get" the typical businessperson. She can't imagine why people would actually enjoy running a company. Hiring people, firing people, telling people that they are not going to get paid because they didn't do a good job. She cannot stand the idea of doing something like that, or being that rough on someone. In business areas like this, Ingrid is like "a fish out of water." She would much prefer having someone do those things for her.

People before Profits

Ingrid has a relatively low profit motive. Don't get me wrong, she is all for making a great income. As a matter of fact, Ingrid is quite well off, thanks to her product sales. But if there is an overwhelming profit, she is quick to share the wealth with friends, family, and employees. Her accountant is convinced Ingrid is overpaying all of her employees.

Under no circumstances would Ingrid ever want to sacrifice quality for profits! I remember sitting in a conference room with Ingrid one day. Her husband, Bill, who ran her company by this point, was giving her an update on the reality of her business. "Costs are going up; our supplier has raised their prices by 30 percent. We're going to have to adjust. I know you want the best quality ingredient, and the highest potency, but either we're going to have to raise our prices, or we're going to have to change the formula."

Tears were streaming down Ingrid's eyes as Bill was delivering the news.

No Innovator wants to be faced with decisions like these. Ingrid didn't want to even think of pricing her customers out of the marketplace. If she had it her way, there would be no scramble for profits—just lots and lots of quality.

"There's Plenty More Where That Came From"

A lot of people claim to be Innovators, because they have come up with great inventions, for example, the kind of stuff you see on late-night infomercials. Okay, you are an inventor at that point, but one thing that differentiates an inventor from an Innovator, like Ingrid, is the Innovation Pipeline. Often, because of that emotional trigger, or whatever interest it was that motivated the Innovator's search for the new product or service, the process of discovery opened the Innovator up to a limitless product pipeline.

Here is an example of a client I worked with back in my business-consulting days. Before he came to us, this Innovator was an active guy. He was a climber, and the typical "weekend warrior" type. Unfortunately, he had a climbing accident, and became a paraplegic.

It was a tough thing to suddenly be sitting in a wheelchair and have to deal with all the pain that goes with adjusting to his new lifestyle. But as he went through the whole healthcare process, he started to realize how tough it was for a paraplegic to do certain everyday activities that many people take for granted. Over time, he ended up developing not just one solution for paraplegic wheelchairs, but a pipeline of close to 20. "I can come up with a hundred more!" he told me one day in a hotel lobby. The emotional trigger sent him on his journey of innovation.

Here is another example. In late 2000, I was running an information technology (IT) company. That fall, while we were in New York City, raising money with some venture capitalists (VCs), we happened to have half a day off. Our contact, who was introducing us to all the bigwigs on Wall Street, offered to take us out to the country and introduce us to one of her other clients. It sure beat sitting in a hotel room for half a day, so we took her up on the offer. We got to meet her client, Michael.

Michael was a physicist who was really passionate about sound. His research had led him to be one of the pioneers of noise-canceling technology. So the next time you put on your noise-canceling headset, you can thank Michael for his innovation. If I recall correctly, he is the original patent holder of part of that technology.

Michael wanted to show us around his office, so we obliged. He took us to a room that was the size of a large conference room. It was full of tables, but there was not a chair in sight. All the tables were full of gadgets, gizmos, and little experimental things.

As I stepped toward one of the tables, I stubbed my toe on what appeared to be a big ugly white box about the size of a suitcase. "Oh, pull that out for me," Michael said as he gestured. "I want to show you something." So I pulled this big white box on wheels out from under the table.

"It's a vacuum cleaner," he claimed. We looked at him somewhat puzzled.

"It looks like a big box with wheels," I said.

"Here, I'll show you how it works." He flipped the power on and sure enough, the big box began to whir and purr like our vacuum cleaner at home. It even began to pick up some bits of lint and dirt off the carpet.

"Watch this," he said as he reached to the back of the box and he flipped another switch.

The vacuum cleaner went silent. Oh, it was still working and picking up knickknacks off the ground, but the whir and purr sound was gone! Now *that* was cool.

He showed us several other inventions and we learned in that short meeting that Michael is the holder of over 600 patents! He is so passionate about his area of expertise that he had tapped a vein of innovation that appears to be endless!

I've had Innovators tell me, "If you can give me a business engine that can do the selling, marketing, and operational stuff for me, I can pretty much build a new product on a daily basis." That's one of the marks of an Innovator.

The Achilles' Heel

You probably already know or have guessed what the Innovator's Achilles' heel is. It's business management!

Too often, Innovators find themselves running their own companies—and it sucks the life right out of them. They end up making some very costly decisions in key areas, like business development and human resources.

I can think of two instances of working with Innovators I had to regretfully walk away from in the last 30 months or so. In both cases, I came to realize that the people they had surrounded themselves with were keeping them from achieving their vision. It is a hard pill to deliver to a passionate and trusting Innovator. "The people you love and trust the most are the reason your company is stuck. You've given them too much power."

In one case, the Innovators (a couple) had a financial partner who literally had no business acumen. He had walked away from a 20-year job with a Fortune 500 company with a nice parachute, but he had no entrepreneurial experience. Every time there was an opportunity to take a step forward in business, this individual would jump up and down and scream in disagreement. After a while of beating my head against a wall, I realized little of what I wanted to do to help their company would be implemented because this Innovator couple had given too much power and control of the decision making to their third partner.

In Ingrid's case, she had 80 percent of the company staffed with family members and friends. Family is great when you are trying to build a corporate culture of trust. However, these individuals were choking the growth potential of the company. There were more politics and watercooler talk in that office of 17 employees than during transition time at the White House. During my tenure with Ingrid's company (keep in mind this was before the BOSI discovery), we restructured the operations of the company to take key family members *out of* executive functions while still giving them an opportunity to be productive and add value. It was not an easy process and there were some tears shed. Even though two key people that needed to be replaced stayed in place (loyalty kept Ingrid from making those changes), looking back, her company is the better for the changes it did go through.

Innovator DNA at Work

Innovators tend to work in bursts. When inspiration comes and all is well emotionally, massive breakthroughs take place. When things aren't quite right mentally and/or emotionally, the Innovation Pipeline comes to a screeching halt.

Most individuals with strong Innovator DNA have a "special place" they go to when they are inspired and ready to produce. For some, it is their local coffee shop. For others, it is a special nook in their home or office. Wherever that special place may be, that is where this individual is typically found.

Innovators do not like to do things that they are not proficient at. It just feels like such a waste of time and valuable energy. Since an Innovator's ego is limited to its area of expertise (be it inventing, writing, cooking, designing, creating, etc.), he or she is very open to let other people do things the Innovator does not like to do.

Innovators are a lot of fun to work for because there is typically no formal job description, performance review, or risk of being fired. Employees who show up, smile, and care about the Innovator's mission typically have tons of job security.

Innovator DNA at Home

Innovator DNA at home is very much like a light bulb. It's either on or it's off. There's really no in-between. When stress or pressure is high, Innovators can be sad, depressed, and reclusive. When all the planets are aligned perfectly and the sun is shining (so to speak), Innovators are in their loving, caring, fun-loving persona. Nothing makes Innovator DNA entrepreneurs happier than to be surrounded by the people they love.

Innovators have a hard time leaving the stress and worries of work at "the office." As a result, much of that emotional burden is transferred to the Innovator's home life, laying the foundation for strife within families. Innovators are very introverted when dealing with stress and worry. In the process, Innovators tend to pull all friends and family members into the funk.

Innovator DNA at Its Best

Hands down, an Innovator is at his or her best when he or she has a breakthrough idea, and the freedom and resources to develop that concept into a prototype. That prototype could be a book concept, a recipe, a gadget, a piece of art, or a formulation. Innovators can get into the zone and accomplish more during this phase than most other BOSI DNAs can accomplish in a lifetime. What takes Innovators a few hours could literally take someone without Innovator DNA months, or even years, to duplicate.

Innovators are also at their best when ensuring product quality. Once a prototype has been produced and delivered to the marketplace, Innovators are obsessively driven by ensuring the same care and quality that went into the prototype is still delivered in the one millionth unit.

Innovator DNA at Its Worst

Put simply, Innovators are at their worst when they are not in the "lab" of the business. Innovators' brilliance is often so off the charts in the area of innovation and creative energy, that almost every other area of business is an area of weakness.

Business strategy, marketing planning and management, finance, supply chain management, sales, and negotiations are just a few of many areas in which Innovators find themselves in a world of hurt. There are specific strategies to protect Innovator DNA entrepreneurs from finding themselves in this position. Those strategies are outlined in the next chapter.

Some Tips on Partnerships and Alliances

Having business partners and marketplace allies are a mission-critical thing for those with Innovator DNA. The higher the Innovator DNA, the more important having business partner(s) becomes. If you have high Innovator DNA, you really don't have a choice but to engage a business partner, key advisor, or CEO to oversee the operations of your business. There is more to be said about that in the next chapter.

Some Typical Statements Made by an Innovator

If you have ever made any of these statements, you have been exhibiting Innovator tendencies. Given your new knowledge about your Entrepreneurial DNA, think about these for a few minutes and see how they fit with your business.

- I didn't really have a grand plan to start a business. I was just doing something I loved and a business grew up around me.

- My no.1 goal in business is to get my product/service to as many people as possible so it can change their lives.
- My no.1 frustration in business is business itself. I am not a businessperson.

> **BOSI BUSINESS STRATEGY ALERT!**
>
> Are you cutting deals with dealers/distributors/resellers hoping that they will do the marketing and selling for you? If set up incorrectly, the tail could end up wagging the dog and your product could end up tarnished in the marketplace.

- I'd much rather be working in the "lab" of my business than in the office or at the cash register.
- Running and managing a business is something that I despise doing. It literally pushes me to a nervous breakdown.
- My mission is so much bigger than I am. It feels like it could take five lifetimes to accomplish what this product/service could do for mankind.
- It frustrates me that my product/service may not reach someone who really needs it because of my business inadequacies.
- Profit is not as important to me as quality. I'd give my product/service away for free if I could.
- People say I'm too trusting of the wrong people.
- Even the thought of raising prices or lowering quality to be "competitive" is overwhelming for me.
- Given the time and freedom, I could invent a whole host of products/services to impact mankind.
- I have a patent-worthy product.
- I would much rather have someone else running my business for me. I don't consider myself business savvy.
- If I had the choice, I'd give up any potential fame and fortune just to have my product help others.
- My family is actively involved in my business with me.

- People say that I am quite gullible around savvy businesspeople.
- I am a trusting person. I tend to give people too much control of my business decisions.

BOSI BUSINESS STRATEGY ALERT!

Do you have an annual sabbatical scheduled into your calendar each year? If not, you are risking more than just your peace of mind. Your innovative mind requires that you step away and recharge your batteries. Your staff and customers will be better off for it.

- My business first started because people loved my product. I would have been happy just to give it to them, but I had to start covering the costs.
- I am loyal to my team members almost to a point of fault.
- I have an advanced degree in my area of expertise.
- People who have tried my product say that it is life-changing.
- I feel honored and privileged to have been given the gift of creating this product.
- I cannot stand hiring, firing, and negotiating. I'd much rather have someone do all that for me.
- I am actually quite happy to admit that I don't know a lot about business.
- I wish I could find a business engine that could take my innovation and get it out to the whole world.

The Innovator DNA at a Glance

STRENGTHS	WEAKNESSES	FRUSTRATIONS
Their Innovation Pipeline is rich and abundant. Given enough time and resources, Innovators can have a museum full of new products.	Business development is not an Innovator's strong suit. Left unchecked, the product/service could die on the vine.	The Innovator didn't really plan to be a business owner so he or she feels quite out of place in the world of entrepreneurship.
Innovators care much more about quality than profits. This can create fanatical customer loyalty for the product/brand.	Innovators tend to lack a "BS" filter. Smooth talkers could convince an Innovator to give up unusual control in the company or technology.	Running and managing a business operation creates significant stress for the Innovator. He or she would much prefer doing research and development (R&D).
Their expertise makes Innovators credible in the marketplace. Investors, employees, and customers are drawn to participate with the Innovator.	Innovators tend to carry other people's burdens. This includes employees and customers. Left unchecked, this can become a source of serious stress and emotional fatigue.	Their innovation (and the mission surrounding it) are much bigger than them. The Innovators fear that the business imbalance could keep their mission from being achieved.

12

Seven Business Optimization Strategies for Innovator DNA

I have a special place in my entrepreneurial heart for the Innovator DNA Profile, so I may come across a bit stronger in this chapter than the others. Just know that it is for a reason.

Innovator DNA gives you a compelling set of gifts that can be leveraged to literally change the world. We learned about those unique strengths in the previous chapter. But we also learned about some compelling weaknesses. This chapter is designed to give you some *actionable strategy* on how to leverage your innate strengths while compensating for your potential weaknesses. Think of it as an optimization process. In some cases, we will be fixing something that is broken. In other cases, we will be taking proactive and precautionary strategies. In a couple of areas, we may not have to do a thing! You may have intuitively taken the necessary optimization steps already.

Being the *chief, cook, and bottle washer* in your company may work for a short window of time when you are starting up your business. However, if you find yourself in that role for months, or even for years, into the process, your ability to reach your mission will be hindered. The seven strategies we will be discussing in this chapter are designed to make sure you achieve your goals and dreams faster and safer than before. The seven strategies we'll discuss are:

- Optimize Your Advisory Board
- Optimize Your Strategic Plan
- Optimize Your Business Model
- Protect Your Intellectual Property
- Optimize Your Work-Life Balance Plan
- Optimize Your Human Resources
- Optimize Your Health and Wellness Plan

Strategy One: Optimize Your Advisory Board

You will be the first to admit that you are not a "business" person, right? So surround yourself with a team of three to five trusted advisors who have a proven business track record. Ask them to be a part of your Advisory Board and help you make key selections and strategic decisions that I'm going to ask you to make in the next few steps.

Here are some tips on how to build your Advisory Board:

1. **Pick people who are not like you:** I'd recommend reading about some of the other BOSI DNAs in this book. Then select at least one Builder and a couple of Specialists to be on this Board. Builders and Specialists will add both business savvy and analytical thought to the Board, and will give you a nice, well-rounded view of business.

    Also add one person you have a longer history with. A best friend, a family member, or a spouse may be a good fit here. You need someone on your Advisory Board who knows you inside and out. This person must be able to tell when you are up and when you are down. Also, this person will be able to give the rest of the Advisory Board insight into what really makes you tick. Most important, he or she will realize when you are falling under the spell of a smooth-talking business partner and will not be afraid to tell you.

2. **Write a nice letter inviting these individuals to your Advisory Board:** Let them know that you would like them to spend a maximum of a couple of hours per month with you (by phone or face to face) to help you with key decisions. I'm going to venture to say that you will get 100 percent of them to say yes.

3. **Once you have your Advisory Board set, ask one of the board members to chair any group meetings:** You don't need a formal meeting schedule. In many cases, you will just be calling each of them individually. They just need to know that when the time comes for you to make big business decisions, that you will call on them to hear you out. The role of the Advisory Board is simply that, to advise you. They should have no decision-making power in your business. Their job is simply to help you think through decisions. You must be the one making the final decision based on how you feel it will impact your mission. Do not give anyone else that power.

Strategy Two: Optimize Your Strategic Plan

Innovators are notorious for not having a structured plan. Their Entrepreneurial DNA tends to be highly creative and fluid, so a structured plan feels like a steel cage. But there is a healthy middle ground between doing what feels good today and having a regimented task list.

Sit down with an expert in strategic planning or business planning. Most Builders will have the innate knack for this. Present your product/service to the expert and let him or her build a strategic plan to get that product to market. Work with the expert to build a three-year plan that will help you and those around you see where your ship is headed and how it is going to get there.

Having that plan will come in handy when you need to source working capital, recruit key staff, or even prepare the company for sale. More importantly, it will help you monitor where the ship is headed on a monthly and quarterly basis.

A good strategic plan will cover:

- Your company's brand position
- Your marketing SPACE funnel (see Appendix A)
- Product offering for the three-year window
- Product pricing (costs and margins)
- Operating plan (how the business will function and grow)
- Financial plan (three-year pro forma financial statements)
- Human resources (HR) plan (who is on your team and how they will operate)
- Exit strategy

You'll have some very big decisions to make during this strategic planning process. Strategy Three dives into one of those areas in more detail. Reading through it will give you an idea of how you should think through the rest of the points in the strategic plan.

Commit to put your strategic plan in place. Without it, your mission will not meet its optimal goal.

Strategy Three: Optimize Your Business Model

As you flesh out your strategic plan, you will find the areas of the business that you want to manage yourself and others that you do not. That will lead you to a crossroad in your business. You will have to make the decision to either plug those holes with full-time employees or outsource to capable firms. This is where your Advisory Board is going to be very valuable. These individuals will help you make the right choice for you and for your enterprise.

When you take a look at your company's operating plan, you'll have to decide whether to staff up internally or look at more of an outsourced model. If you are the only owner in the business, I would strongly advise you to consider more of an outsourced model because that means less management headaches for you in-house. In this case, you need to find companies that can get things done that you would normally have in-house employees doing, for example:

- Production, inventory management, and fulfillment
- Order taking and order processing
- Information technology (IT) services
- Marketing
- Social media, search engine optimization (SEO), and search engine marketing (SEM)
- Public relations (PR)
- Finance and accounting

I can assure you that there are companies—regionally, nationally, and internationally—who specialize in all these areas. Depending on what your company's business needs are, you can pick and choose which services you need. This way, you can hire one full-time right-hand person who can manage all those vendors and allow you to focus on your gifting of innovation and research and development (R&D).

If you are fortunate enough to have a trustworthy business partner who has some Builder and/or Specialist DNA in him or her, you may be in luck. This individual should handle the day-to-day oversight of the business, so you don't have to. It will also open up the option of using hired, in-house talent rather than outsourcing.

Either way, my point is that you need to protect yourself, the Innovator, from having to manage a business operation. Whether you outsource the headache or bring in a partner to handle the headache for you, it is really up to you and your Advisory Board

Strategy Four: Protect Your Intellectual Property

Your Intellectual Property (IP) is who you are. It defines you and it's what you live and breathe. Don't give it to anyone—not even your own company. There are ways to set up your IP so that it is always owned and controlled by you. This way, if the unfortunate happens and your business enterprise itself fails, you can still retain the most important part of the business, your IP.

Take your key advisor and sit down with an IP lawyer. Let the lawyer know that you want to look at all the ways to best protect your IP. Don't settle for the lawyer's "best" recommendation. Ask him or her to give you good, better, and best-case scenarios. Then take that information back to your Advisory Board to discuss with them, and then you make the best decision for you.

Strategy Five: Optimize Your Work-Life Balance Plan

Unlike some other BOSI DNAs, you were not built to burn the candle at both ends for an extended period of time. You carry emotion—from yourself, your family, and even your clients—along with you every day. If you do not have a systematic plan in place that gives you the opportunity to vent and detoxify your brain, you will have a nervous breakdown. That is what is interesting to me as I study the various BOSI DNAs. The other BOSI DNAs have a high potential for heart attacks, if they don't adjust. Innovators, on the other hand, have a higher propensity for potential nervous breakdowns and emotional issues.

Set a plan to go away from your business for a continuous window of time each year. I'd like to recommend that you start with a 14-day sabbatical and try to extend it to as high as 90 days in the next few years. You need that time to rest, recover, rejuvenate, and refresh the Innovator in you. Think of things you really love to do. Take a cruise, go sit on a beach, go pet some sea lions, or serve in a ministry. Do something that takes you away from your core business. Do something that takes you away from giving yourself away—even if for just a short window of time.

I'd also like to recommend that you take someone along on your sabbatical who can cater to your needs and make sure you don't have to stress over where to eat, what to do, and how to pay for things. I bet you have someone like that in your life. Take that person with you.

"Joe, I just can't see myself taking the time this year. Things are really busy," you may say.

Don't give me that mumbo jumbo, I'm not buying it. If you really care about your mission, you will go away. I've seen too many Innovators burn out at the most completely inopportune time, and I'd rather have you skip that unfortunate demise. If you burn out, so does your mission because nobody else on your team can do what you do. Make sure your business partner and advisors read this section of the book. They need to know how to best care for and serve you.

Schedule the time right now for the next calendar year and make the commitment to get away. Your mission demands it.

Strategy Six: Optimize Your Human Resources

If you already have employees (or helpers) in your business, my guess is they are your friends and family members. You already know the good side of having them on your team. They are trustworthy. But here is the bad side. Many times the Innovator doesn't hire people to match the *mission*, the Innovator hires people to match the *emotion*.

So someday, when the opportunity presents itself for you to really change the world, my question to you is this:

"Will the family and friends who are part of your business have the expertise, track record, and ability to run and operate a much larger company?"

If the answer is no (and it usually is), then let's put systems in place so nobody is disappointed later. For the loved ones in your business, let's give them a place to work and earn an income. Let's make sure the income is fair. Then, leave room in the business structure for highly talented experts who can be hired down the road who can actually help you achieve your long-term mission.

The mistake I have seen a lot of Innovators make is they paint a picture for friends and family that leads those individuals to believe that they will be part of the company's executive management team forever. Is that really the best thing for your company and for your mission? The last thing you want is to have your friends and family unknowingly sabotage your company, just to keep it from growing, so that it doesn't outgrow them. Trust me, I've seen it happen too many times with clients I love. I don't want it to happen to you. Put the systems in place now for human resources if you have chosen to have an in-house employee base.

Strategy Seven: Optimize Your Health and Wellness Plan

The fact is, if you're not making a concerted effort to become healthier every day, your mission to change the world with your innovation is at grave risk. Chances are, with the amount of stress and emotion you carry around, you'll have a nervous breakdown as your business starts to really grow.

Too many company founders wait until they get "the news" from their doctor before they step into a wellness journey. You may have already received "the news." But maybe, just maybe, I'm catching you *before* things progress that far.

I've had the joy of watching clients make the decision to adopt a wellness-focused lifestyle. Those who do embrace the journey feel energetic, vibrant, mentally acute, physically fit, and ready to take on the world. How are you feeling today?

The journey to feeling the way those clients feel does not have to be cumbersome, inconvenient, or painful. It's just a matter of taking simple, daily steps that will help you become more effective and reach your mission safer. Find a great health and wellness program and plug into it. Unlike most entrepreneurs, you are quite irreplaceable in your company, so you have a responsibility to keep yourself around for as long as possible.

Factoring In Your Secondary DNAs

There is a chance you have a Secondary Specialist DNA or Opportunist DNA in your BOSI Profile. It is fairly rare for an Innovator to have any strong Builder DNA. If there is any Builder DNA in you, it's probably just a smidgen. Here's some insight into some nuances of the additional DNA in you.

Specialist DNA

Read a little about the Specialist and you will see how easy it is for this DNA to get stuck working on the details of his or her business. That tendency is heightened with your Primary Innovator DNA. If you have Innovator-Specialist DNA, you absolutely must ensure that you surround yourself with a team of capable managers and team members. They will be able to operate and grow the business around you.

Specialist DNA also means you probably have a lot of credibility in your area of expertise. It is important that you leverage that expertise by highlighting it in the marketplace. A good pay-for-placement public relations (PR) firm will be able to get your story and discovery to the media. The press is always looking for breakthrough ideas, concepts, and products to talk about. Your discovery could be next.

With Innovator-Specialist DNA, business development and marketing is the no. 1 weakness. To combat that, consider retaining a business development advisor to help guide you and your Advisory Board through the strategic decisions of how to take your product or service to market.

Opportunist DNA

The Innovator-Opportunist (IO) is a right-quadrant combination. This means you will have a virtually unlimited capacity to conceptualize and invent new things. Your Secondary Opportunist DNA draws you to concepts that are big (and fast) moneymakers. Your Primary Innovator DNA will draw you to concepts that serve a greater good. This could result in some confusion and frustration, but the Innovator DNA in you will typically win out in those circumstances.

The Innovator-Opportunist DNA combination tends to love being in environments rich in camaraderie, fun, and positive energy. It has a very hard time surviving in authoritative, stoic environments. Make sure the corporate culture you set, and the people you surround yourself with, fit the type of environment you thrive in.

The gift of creativity present in this DNA combination is matched by a weakness of being quite disorganized. Important tasks often get left undone. Follow-up is typically very weak. If this is an area of weakness for you, hire an administrator who can manage those repetitive tasks.

Put systems in place to make sure a red flag goes up when you start chasing an idea that is not part of your core strategic plan. The Opportunist's ability to dream up ideas and the Innovator's ability to make them a reality is risky to the focus of your core business. To offset any weaknesses of this DNA combination, make sure you have some Builder and Specialist advisors, partners, or employees.

Builder DNA

Although quite rare, I have occasionally found Innovator DNA entrepreneurs with some Builder DNA. This is a highly desirable profile since it is a cross-quadrant relationship. The weaknesses of one DNA are the strengths of the other. What makes this DNA combination so compelling is the ability to build breakthrough products and deliver them in a scalable way to the marketplace. No other BOSI DNA has that innate gift.

When you look at some of the most talked about brands in the marketplace—like Apple, Google and Kodak—they are all based on an Innovator-Builder DNA combination. Your venture has the potential to be a global breakthrough organization based on your DNA.

Take an inventory of your desire for business management. Chances are, since your Innovator score is higher than your Builder score, you'd much rather be the research and development person than the business manager. You would do well to have an in-house management team who is executing the game plan that you have built. You may feel tempted to get hands-on in the management and operation of your business. However, just know that the more profitable scenario is for you to hire people to do the business management for you. Your expertise in R&D is irreplaceable.

Summary

Innovators thrive when surrounded by capable advisors and team members. Take a good hard look at the Entrepreneurial DNA of the people surrounding you and make any necessary adjustments to optimize that team. Innovators also thrive when business development and/or business management is in someone else's hands. Consider which of those options are a better fit for you. The BOSI Web site has free tools and resources you can use to qualify members of your Advisory Board, mastermind team, and peer group. When given the opportunity to be creative—without the stress and headaches of business management—Innovators build and deliver breakthrough products and services to the marketplace and have a huge impact on people's lives.

The Action Plan Checklist

Here is a quick action planner you can use to start the process of moving to deploy some of the strategies you have learned. You may choose to skip one or more strategies because you have intuitively optimized them already.

Optimization Points	Priority (1-7)	Start Date	Resources/People Needed
Optimize Your Advisory Board			
Optimize Your Strategic Plan			
Optimize Your Business Model			
Protect Your Intellectual Property (IP)			
Optimize Your Work-Life Balance Plan			
Optimize Your Human Resources			
Optimize Your Health and Wellness Plan			

part three

Building Your Strategic Plan

Would you believe it if I told you that we are two-thirds of the way through our journey together? We are now getting into the most important third of the book where we get to take what you've learned earlier and use it to construct a new strategic plan for your business based on your Entrepreneurial DNA. We'll begin by looking at the key building blocks of a strong strategic plan and then construct your plan using those building blocks.

We are going to focus on seven key exercises. Each exercise builds on the previous one. So take the time to do each exercise, but do so in the order in which they are laid out for you. Only equity stakeholders and key advisors in your company should do Exercises One, Two, and Three. You'll see why as we go through the exercises.

The purpose of the first three exercises is to go back to basics and set up a foundational set of filters that will root out and protect against "free radicals"—pieces of stray strategy or decisions that looked good on the surface but go against your Entrepreneurial DNA. Exercises Four, Five, Six, and Seven are an opportunity for you to bring the rest of your team into the picture. So if you are a Builder, this is where you bring in any contracted experts or your upper-management team. If you are an Opportunist, you definitely want your coach to go through the exercises with you. If you are a Specialist, this would be a great opportunity for you to put your marketing firm to the test. If you are an Innovator, you shouldn't even consider doing these exercises without your advisor (or advisory team) there to guide you through this process.

Without the right filters in place, a well-intentioned entrepreneur could make changes to his or her business that could be devastating. When we do the brand positioning exercise, you are going to discover *who* your target audience is. You are going to learn to listen to that very specific group of people in your marketplace so that you stay on course, servicing *their* needs. However, you will also learn to ignore the noisemakers that were never supposed to be your customers in the first place.

These first three exercises also serve another significant purpose. As you make operational, HR, and business development decisions in Exercises Four, Five, Six, and Seven, the results of the first three foundational exercises will act as filters through which you will make go and no-go decisions.

QUICK ALERT: Don't lose sight of the discovery you have already made about your Entrepreneurial DNA. Let that discovery drive the decisions you make in these exercises. I'll remind you about this as we get into Exercise Four, but keep this in mind even as you lay the foundation in Exercises One, Two, and Three.

chapter

13

Setting the Foundation of Your New Strategic Plan

In the human body, free radicals, if left unchecked, can lead to harmful diseases. Your business is no different. Stray strategic or tactical decisions, made over time and allowed to hang around, can also cause significant harm. They need to be removed *before* we start building new strategy.

Sources of Free Radicals

Before we proceed, I'll highlight the four *sources* of free radicals that may occur in your business.

The Buffet of Business Strategy

Put simply, it is all the different sources of input you get—from seminars and books to workshops and networking groups. You go all over the country, the world, and the Web searching for "best practices" in marketing, HR, finance, business planning, and funding. You sit at one chamber event. Then you go and read some guru's marketing book. Then you go to another guru's negotiating seminar. You are collecting new content every day.

It's no different than walking into a buffet restaurant. You are hungry and its lunchtime, so you end up trying a little bit of the American fare. But since there's still some room on your plate, you try a little bit of the Chinese spread. For a second serving, you have some Italian and top it off with the Japanese stuff. Then there is that salad island and, of course, don't forget the dessert bar. Forty-five minutes later, you feel overloaded, overbloated, tired, and very lethargic. Businesses feel the same way when they've been taken to the buffet of business strategy. Don't get me wrong. Many of these strategies are probably pretty smart and good strategies on their own. But when you combine them with certain others, they start to conflict and they don't align well. They start to cause all kinds of challenges in the business.

There are a lot of entrepreneurs out there who are trying a little bit of this and a little bit of that, and as a result, they are not seeing healthy results. That's because they are sabotaging their business by not being more selective on what they allow *into* their business.

Internal Forces

Internal forces include *people* like staff, business partners, strategic partners, and managers in your business. Every human being *internal* to your business brings a certain culture to the business. Some bring a very positive culture that moves the business forward. Some bring a not-so-positive culture. You need to be extra-cautious of internal forces that you inherit. For example, many entrepreneurs buy into an existing business only to find internal forces working against them. They buy a business and Suzy Q, the office manager, is inherited as part of the transaction. Suzy Q may have been there for 20 years, and she probably plans to be there for the next 20. Chances are, there are mind-sets and systems she is carrying from the previous business or the previous ownership that are not optimum for *your* Entrepreneurial DNA.

Going through the upcoming exercises will help you identify and fix those differences.

External Forces

Competitors and customers are examples of the external forces that can impact how your company operates. All too often, entrepreneurs make significant strategic changes in business around what competitors are doing.

You see competitor no. 1 roll out a certain marketing plan and you try to copy it. You see competitor no. 2 make a product launch and you make adjustments in your sales systems to compensate for that product launch. Sometimes that decision is a necessary evil, but very often the decision is tactical, but doesn't tie into your longer-term strategy or into your Entrepreneurial DNA. Before you know it, you are two degrees, five degrees, or sometimes twenty degrees off course and quite a bit down the road before you realize that you are nowhere near your destination.

Prospects

Prospects can be another source of free radicals. I see a lot of entrepreneurs make the mistake of listening to the *wrong* audience. A disgruntled first-time buyer may call in and give you a piece of his or her mind or post a not-so-flattering comment on your Web site. Essentially, he or she says something to the effect of: "If you'd just do this differently and that differently, I'd be your customer for life." Without the proper filters in place, an entrepreneur could make the costly mistake of making changes for the sake of the wrong customer—thereby creating a free radical of strategy in the business.

Exercise One: The Paper Napkin

Let's get started with Exercise One, The Paper Napkin. From 2005 to 2007, we lived in southwest Houston, Texas. In my home office was a black picture frame that I was holding for a friend who was traveling internationally. Behind the glass of this frame sat a torn-out page from a spiral-bound sketchbook. People would stare at that picture frame and assume it was the proud father in me trying to memorialize my four-year-old's latest preschool creation. A couple of people though, took the time to look at the right-hand corner for a pleasant (and fairly shocking) surprise. The signature wasn't that of my four-year-old, but rather of Picasso. Needless to say, that picture frame hanging in my home office dramatically boosted the value of my home for the time that it hung there. That rough sketch was the "paper napkin" that ended up being the inspiration and planning behind a priceless Picasso painting.

I want to visit with you about *your* original sketch, the original vision you had for your business. I want to take you back to the *paper napkin* where your business was born.

Here is why: Somewhere in the simplicity and passion of your paper napkin is the secret to your company's explosive growth. That may sound crazy as you are reading these words, but you will see I'm right as you go through these exercises with me.

Let me make sure that you know what I mean by your "paper napkin." It is the piece of paper, digital file, or literally a paper napkin you used when you originally came up with your business idea. Do you remember the day you came up with your business idea? You may have to go back years. There is a chance that the actual document is sitting in a landfill somewhere. However, I can guarantee that this document's contents are engraved in your memory.

So here is what you may have to do. You may have to take some time today, and retreat to a quiet place for a minimum of 30 minutes. Grab a couple of clean sheets of paper and a pen with blue ink. Then, in your mind's eye, go back to the beginning, where this all started. Start to lay out for me, and with me, your original business concept.

Review of Your Paper Napkin

Now, if you already have your paper napkin, dig it out and revisit it. As you review (or reconstruct) your paper napkin, I want to ask you a series of simple *what, how,* and *why* questions.

I'm here to tell you this is the most important fundamental step to building a huge and fulfilling business. Don't skip this step or shortcut it in any way. Ready? Here goes.

What was the original movie playing in your mind the day you decided to start this business?

- What was the original product or service?
- Who was your target audience going to be?
- What was the business model you had in mind?
- What were some of your original marketing ideas?
- How did you originally plan to find customers?
- How was your product or service priced originally? Why?
- Did you see yourself as the sole owner or having business partners? Why?
- What kinds of employees were going to be working for you?
- What did they look like in your original movie? How did they dress, interact, work, and play?
- What were your customers going to be like?
- Why were people going to buy from you?
- What would customers be saying about you in the marketplace?
- What was going to make you unique in the marketplace?
- Why were people going to buy from you and not from your competition?
- What was your vision for the business two years from its start-up, five years from its start-up, or ten years from its start-up?
- Why did you start the business in the first place? What was the burning desire in you?

I want to take you back to the original intent behind the business so you can take an inventory of what has changed since then. I'm going to say that again. The reason I want to take you back to the original intent, the reason we are going to spend time on your paper napkin is so that we can figure out what has changed since then.

What is different today?

- Are you doing the day-to-day things you envisioned yourself doing when you first started this company, or are you caught up in activities today that you don't really enjoy doing?
- Are you working with the kinds of people you've always intended to work with, or are you working with some not so attractive personalities who found their way into your company?
- Are the people that surround you as motivated, passionate, and loyal as you expected?
- Are your prospects responding to your marketing and sales efforts the way you planned, or is it an uphill battle?
- Are your customers loyal and fanatical about what you do and what you provide them, just like you planned?
- Are your customers responsive to your offers, or do they shop the competition?

When you compare your *original vision* to your *current reality*, here's my question, What do you find? Do you find yourself saying:

> "Well, Joe, you know what? I really didn't have a clue when I started my business, but I've really learned a lot and I've exceeded and outperformed my original vision. Things are better than I ever imagined they would be."

Or are you saying:

> "Well, Joe, when I really think about it, I thought we'd be much further along by now in the process. I thought we'd be doing so much better. Things aren't where I want them to be. I've got some good people, but they're not ideal. I've got happy customers, but they're not fanatical. Things are good, but they're not great."

Or maybe you find yourself quite a bit off course and saying:

"You know Joe, things started off well but somewhere along the way, we took an extra left turn somewhere or drove too fast past an exit. The bottom line is, I'm frustrated that we aren't anywhere near the destination I had set."

Regardless of which group you find yourself in, the first step to building a highly successful growth plan for the future is to go back to your *original* growth plan. Some of the best ideas for growth don't come from consultants and high-priced experts; you have already *had* their ideas. Take the time right now to draw out or revisit your original paper napkin. And if you do this step correctly, you are going to find yourself getting excited again. Your heart is going to start to race as your heartbeat starts to pick up. You are going back to the core of what your business was really supposed to be.

Areas of Business Better or Worse Than Paper Napkin

The final step in this exercise is to highlight the areas of your business that are *better today* compared to your paper napkin and the areas that are *worse today* compared to your paper napkin. Answer the series of questions that follow and document those areas that are better or worse in the box on page 200. This list is going to come in handy as we move through the strategic planning process.

The Good

- What have you learned about your target audience that you didn't know when you started?
- What improvements have you made in how you attract, convert, and retain customers? What systems have you put in place that were not part of the paper napkin, and have helped the business?
- Who are the people who have come on-board your team that fit the picture you had in mind as ideal team members?

The Not-So-Good

- Are there some processes that have found their way into your business that just don't make sense anymore?
- Are there some systems that just slow things down and are not efficient anymore?
- Are there some people who have made it "on to the bus," to use Jim Collins's metaphor, but who need to be vacated in order for your business to get to the next level?
- Are there some mind-sets about customers, competition, growth, or risk that need to be replaced in order for you to get to the next level?
- Is there a reputation that has been built up about you in the marketplace through your customers or competitors that needs to be changed before your business can go to the next level?
- What are some of the free radicals that your business has picked up along the way that it must absolutely get rid of?

Areas of Business Better or Worse Today

The Good	The Not-So-Good

Exercise Two: Vision and Mission

In this exercise, we are going to build your company's internal and external vision and mission. Here is why. Your brand is a rudderless ship without it. A lost brand leads to weak marketing. Weak marketing leads to low sales conversion. Low sales conversion leads to a cascading series of events that are quite unpleasant.

The purpose of this exercise is to build a matrix that becomes an active filter in your decision making at the office. Done right, this filter will drive what types of employees you hire, what types of products you release, and how you run your company operations. Believe it or not, all those initiatives feed from this vision and mission.

If you go to the marketing brochure or Web site of most companies, you'll see a mission statement the sales manager seemingly crafted two hours before the brochure masters were due at the printer. The mission statement says something along the lines of: "We are here to serve our customers and add value . . . *blah, blah* . . . integrity, honesty, fairness . . . *blah, blah* . . . community service."

I'd like to suggest that there is a more functional vision and mission you can craft for your company. I want you to build a vision and mission that will act as a *catalyst* for the right activities and a *barrier* to the wrong ones. I must credit my good friend Gordon Dodd, in the United Kingdom, for teaching me this exercise that I now want to pass on to you. Here is the definition:

Vision is the largest understanding of what your business is about and what it can deliver. Mission is the means by which you're going to attain it.

Let me show you how vision and mission play out in real life. Then we'll dive into the exercise.

I'm going to talk to you about General Dwight ("Ike") David Eisenhower, who later became President Eisenhower. The big *vision* set by Eisenhower as the Supreme Allied Commander was "the complete and utter overthrow of the German Third Reich." Now, that was the *vision* at his level of leadership. This meant that all work that was ever done had to be filtered through this concept. If this did not occur, then the operation, the research, or the training were not undertaken.

The largest scale *mission* set out by General Ike was Operation Overlord (D-Day) on June 6, 1944. It had one purpose—"to secure a beachhead from which to begin the ground assault on the German Third Reich." This was the *mission* that facilitated the bigger *vision*.

For a series of cascading senior officers down the line, D-Day was their *vision*, with their own *mini-mission* required to achieve it all the way down the line to the rifleman whose *vision* was "to successfully land and secure a position." The rifleman's *mission* was set relative to the senior officer's bigger *vision*. Effectively a series of interlocking *vision statements* and *mission statements* guaranteed General Ike that he could deliver from the highest level of his *vision* all the way down to the detail on the ground.

Again, the *vision* was "the complete and utter overthrow of the German Reich." The *mission* on that day was "to secure the beachhead."

Vision is what you want to accomplish at the highest level.
Mission is how you're going to get there.

How Internal Vision and Mission Work Together

Let's say I wanted to plan a trip to my favorite vacation spot. Let's also say that my wife reminds me of the need for us to be good stewards of our resources. Given those two situations, my *internal vision* becomes "to vacation in Maui for a reasonable price."

The *internal mission* will force me to ask *how* I'm going to achieve that *vision*. I could plan ahead. I could keep our dates flexible. I may even look at several discounts and packages online. So if my *internal vision* is "to get there for a reasonable price," my *internal mission* then becomes "to plan ahead, keep flexible dates, and shop for discounts and packages." Do you see where I'm going with this?

Building Your Internal Vision

Now, how does this apply to you as a business owner and chief executive officer (CEO)? Well, you have an *internal vision* for your business. Chances are, your *internal vision* isn't about shipping 50 cases of product today or having 60 customers walk through the door tomorrow. If we were to look at your paper napkin, you've got a grand vision. Your *internal vision* is much bigger than what is about to happen this week, this month, this quarter, or even this year.

Take a look at Table 13-1. This is a sample vision and mission from an architectural firm.

Table 13-1   Sample Vision and Mission

Internal Vision	External Vision
To design great buildings and spaces within a successful commercial business	To exceed clients' expectations every time
Internal Mission	External Mission
To attain total commitment and to search for quality from brief to completion, for all clients	To deliver great buildings and consultancy services every time, on time and on budget

In the left column, you see the internal vision and the internal mission. In the right column, you see the external vision and the external mission. Your *internal vision* is about *you*. What are *you* looking to accomplish with your business? This is *not* about your customers.

In the case of the architectural firm, they said they want "to design great buildings and spaces within a successful commercial business." Let me give you a couple of other examples for an *internal vision*.

- A physician's practice said their *internal vision* was "to give caring and effective care within a profitable chain of locations." That is why they exist: "to give caring and effective care while staying profitable and scalable."
- At BOSI, our own *internal vision* is "to be the trusted source of insight and support to the world of entrepreneurship." So that is why we exist. That is who we want to be when we grow up. That is the vision I have cast for my team.

Go back to your paper napkin now and ask yourself, "What is my internal vision?" I'm going to recommend you jot down four, five, or even ten variations of what you think your *internal vision* could be. Then start to refine it down. Your *internal vision* is a summary of the visions you crafted on your paper napkin.

Building Your Internal Mission

In the case of BOSI, if our *internal vision* is "to be the trusted source of insight and support to the world of entrepreneurship," I have to ask myself *how* that is going to happen. The answer is "by creating breakthrough success–generating solutions and delivering them profitably to our users." That is BOSI's *internal mission*.

Take a look at the architectural firm's *internal vision* and *internal mission*. See how they connect together. The *vision* sets the "what we are." The *mission* sets the "how we'll get it done." They believe that if they "had total commitment and search for quality from proposal to completion for every client," then they would end up with "great buildings and spaces." Does this make sense? One leads to the other.

Let's take a quick peek at the *internal vision* and *internal mission* of the physician's practice to make sure you've got this down to a science. The physician's practice can test the output and say, "Okay, if we focused on quality standards, the latest technology, and excellent follow–up, would we be providing caring and effective care to our patients?" Yes. Okay, great, then that's probably a solid *internal mission* to fit the *internal vision*.

Now let's talk about you. How will your *internal vision* become a reality? The *how* is what your *internal mission* becomes. So again, jot down four to five variations of what you believe your *internal mission* could be. Then challenge, reduce, and refine your list down to a single statement that fits the formula we've discussed so far.

QUICK ALERT: This is the perfect time for me to offer a quick word of caution. Experience has shown that this is one of the few exercises that many entrepreneurs skip past or race through. They think, "Okay, I get it. I get it. Let's move on to the next thing." Please don't do that. This exercise is the absolute bedrock to sound strategy. This is the foundation on which your entire brand and marketing strategy will sit. Trust me when I tell you this will be one of the new tools in your CEO toolbox that you will use a lot this year.

It will help you decide which types of deals to get involved with, what types of people to hire, where your brand positions itself, and how to market yourself. So, take the time right now. Define your *internal vision* and *internal mission*.

External Vision and External Mission

Now, let's talk about your *external vision* and *external mission*. If your *internal vision* was about *you* or what you are about, the *external vision* as you can imagine is about *your customer*. What is the impact your business is going to have on them? What is in it for them? What is the economic, social, personal, or emotional impact you or your business will have on the external marketplace? That is the external vision.

So in the architectural firm's case, their *external vision* is "to exceed clients' expectations every time." That is simple, yet powerful. As you can see, none of this needs to be rocket science or be worthy of a Pulitzer prize. If you like the architectural firm's *external vision*, take it! Just make sure to weigh it against your paper napkin and ensure it is what you are really about. The physician's practice says their *external vision* is "to facilitate healing and recovery for our patients."

At BOSI, our *external vision* is "to have our users in a better place than before we met them." This means that whether you read one of our books, attend an event, or just use the free tools on our Web site, we have a vision for you. We are obligated to make sure you leave the experience better off than before you met us. That gives us a measuring stick by which to hold ourselves accountable.

So what is your *external vision*? What is it that you want your clients, your customers, or your world to experience through your being in business? Jot down four or five different thoughts and then refine them down.

The final piece is easy now that you have the formula down. We are looking to build an external mission. We have set an *external vision* (what we want for our customer). Now we have to answer how we are doing to ensure it happens. Take a look at the architectural firm's *external vision* and *external mission*, and use it as a guide to build your own.

Once you have refined and reduced your vision statement and mission statement, put them in the box that follows.

Vision Statement and Mission Statement

Internal Vision	External Vision
Internal Mission	External Mission

Now set this vision and mission statement exercise aside. Set a reminder on your calendar to come back to your notes a week from now. Then ask yourself, "Do these notes resonate with me?" Hold your paper napkin next to it and ask, "Do these two documents match up?" Your goal is to look at the big picture you crafted in your paper napkin and see it come to life in your internal vision and your internal mission. Complete this exercise and I can assure you that you are miles ahead of your competition when it comes to setting a course for a more profitable and enjoyable entrepreneurial journey.

Exercise Three: The Market Positioning

Now we get to one of my favorite exercises, the market positioning exercise. Long before customer service kicks into high gear and orders get taken. Before sales teams do their windshield time and marketing departments figure out what the year's advertising plan is going to look like. Before the business plan is even written, your brand and market positioning should be determined. Your brand is not about colors, logo design, and name selection. As I mentioned earlier, brand is the *ethos* of a business.

Let me explain. You and I have an identity as people. We have our beliefs, our philosophy about life, our approach to living, our political persuasions, our spiritual convictions, our family heritage, where we choose to live, where we choose to eat, and how we choose to dress. All these things define and reflect our identity—our personal brand.

You have probably noticed that there are people out there who never took the time to do their personal brand positioning. As a result, they just go about life and pick up belief systems, lifestyle choices, and eating habits on a whim. I'll even go out on a limb to suggest that most people don't really know who they *are* and who they *are not*. You don't get to discover what their brand is until you hear their eulogy or read the carefully crafted words on their tombstone. I guess when you think about it, most people's personal brand isn't truly identified until they are in a hole in the ground.

Unfortunately, the same is true of 90 percent of entrepreneurial ventures. Entrepreneurs sweep this whole process under the rug and go, "Oh, yeah branding. We'll do it later once we've hired a marketing person."

Then, years later, these entrepreneurs sit in their corner offices frustrated as to why their companies have unmotivated salespeople or frustrated customers. These entrepreneurs fret over having to deal with pricing wars and competitors who are growing faster. They grumble about having trouble standing out in a crowd of competitors in the marketplace.

To keep you from being one of those frustrated entrepreneurs, we are going to do this exercise together. The final output of this process is a one-page description of who *you are* as a company, and who *you are not*. Think of it as a eulogy being said about your business on the day of your company's birth (or rebirth), rather than on the day of its demise.

This exercise combines market positioning with some basic brand positioning. Credit for this exercise goes to a brilliant brand strategist, Rod Connor, who is the founder of Branded Sports Group in England. I don't consider this exercise the complete brand positioning process, so please know that there is much more you need to do when creating your brand position. However, this exercise does do a pretty good job of market positioning while touching on some key brand elements. This is why I have chosen to share this it with you.

I am going to take you through a series of seven questions, so I'd suggest you grab your journal, laptop, or legal pad. As we go through each question, I recommend you write down *every* word that comes to your mind. In other words, don't try and refine things yet. Just write down everything that comes to your mind. Like an active brainstorming session, more is better in this case. At the end of the session, you can come back to capture, reduce, and refine the answers to look like the examples you are about to see.

If we do this right, you will be able to hand the finished product to a future employee, a shareholder, a graphic designer, an IT programmer, an ad agency, a PR company, or a marketing company. They will be able to read through the finished product in two to three minutes to get a rich and multidimensional picture of your company. So with that said, let's jump into the market and brand positioning exercise.

Question One: The Company Target—Who is the person and what is the situation for which your company is always the best choice?

When I ask the typical financial planner, real estate agent, or pizza shop owner this question for the first time, I get the same answer, "Everyone!"

Then I take them back to two operative words in the question above. The first word is *and*. The second word is *always*. Read the question again while adding an extra inflection to those two words and see if it changes your response from "everyone" to something more targeted than that.

Below are examples of how a couple of big boys—McDonald's and Days Inn—answer this question:

McDonald's: *People who can relate to childhood happiness*
Parents who want to treat their kids
Kids who want to have fun with their meal
Days Inn: *People traveling by car who just want a*
good room for one night

Take a look at McDonald's company target. They feel there are three types of people *and* situations for which McDonald's is *always* the right choice.

Isn't Days Inn's position impressive? I thought it was. They have refined their target down to people who fit a specific profile. Because of this highly refined target, they are able to cater everything—from their location selection and operating plan to advertising strategy—around it. They aren't wasting resources trying to appeal to people on their honeymoon or corporate convention. By identifying the perfect person *and* situation for which your company is *always* the best choice, you are going to set a culture around which your marketing, sales, and operations will take place.

Take a couple of minutes to jot down some thoughts about your company target. Use active brainstorming to jot down everything that comes to mind. You may fill up a half page to a full page. That's a good thing. Describe these individuals (or companies) in as much detail as you can.

Question Two: Company Insight—What insight do you have into the target audience's needs, wants, values, and attitudes?

Since we have identified the target audience in Question One, now we are asking the question about what we know *about* these consumers. What do we know about their lifestyles, beliefs, frustrations, habits, pastimes, and more? Here is an example of how Coke answers this question:

Coke: *People looking to be refreshed and energized*

Coke says, "What we know about our consumer is they want to be refreshed and energized." So what do you know about your customers? What can you say are their wants and needs?

If you are a business-to-business (B2B) company, what are the frustrations of your consumers? What do you know about them? Don't limit yourself to the frustrations that just apply to the solutions you provide. Get a multidimensional picture of the audience and include areas you may not even touch.

If you are a business-to-consumer (B2C) company, what do you know about the consumers? What do they look, act, and talk like? When I do this exercise with an entrepreneur, we end up with a half page to a full page of content. Most of it ends up in the trash later. But along the way, we end up picking up some nuggets that truly give us insight into who we are out to serve. So if a silly thought pops in your mind, write it down anyway. *Small hinges open big doors.* That silly idea may just be one of those small hinges.

Question Three: Reason to Believe—How is your company better than the competition? Who recommends it, which opinion leaders swear by it, and who sponsors and associates themselves with it?

Put another way, the question I am asking here is: What credibility does your company carry that's going to give a prospect confidence to move forward with your brand? Here are examples of how Rolex and Levis answer this question:

Rolex: *Worn by the world's highest achievers*
Levis: *Worn by style leaders the world over, 1854 heritage*

Start to list your answers to these questions.

- Who recommends your brand?
- What opinion leaders swear by it?
- Who sponsors it?
- Who associates themselves with your company and your brand with pride?
- Are there celebrities who have tried your product and loved it?
- Are there key opinion leaders or large companies that have partnered with you?

Imagine you and I are sitting down across from someone who fits the target audience we identified in Question One. They are asking:

"Well, why should I believe in your brand? There are seven other brands to choose from. What is more credible about your brand that isn't true about the others?"

Rolex says, "Our watches are worn by the world's highest achievers." See, Rolex did something brilliant. They identified a target audience (high achievers). They then dug into the needs, wants, and desires of that audience. They found that the audience of high achievers likes to be recognized as such. So they built their brand around ensuring that the top achievers in sports, entertainment, and business were using their product. Now when a young financial planner or real estate agent hits the million-dollar club for the first time, they associate that achievement with a Rolex. They are more apt to join the fraternity of Rolex owners because it makes them feel a certain way.

Levis is worn by style leaders around the world. Levis has identified the reason to believe in their brand. They know that teeny-boppers, college students, and wannabe style leaders like me will engage with the Levis brand because of the real-style leaders (rock stars, celebrities, super-athletes) who wear them too.

If you are a business-to-business (B2B) company, you are going to have some very specific reasons why someone is going to partner with your brand over some other brand.

QUICK ALERT: I want you to understand that we are talking about a *potential* customer of your company. This is somebody looking to possibly do business with you. What is going to push that person over the fence? What credibility can you give that potential customer that will make him or her think, "Oh, if so-and-so is using you or if Expert X has endorsed or aligned with you, then who am I to argue with your credibility?"

The classic sign that a company has not done this step is when you walk into their business and it's all about price and service. "We've got the best prices in town," says the coupon mailer. "Service is our cornerstone," claims their *Yellow Pages* ad.

Ugh! I say. Build the right brand, and you will not have to compete on price or make service your *not-so-unique* selling proposition.

Question Four: Discriminator—What is the single-most compelling and competitive reason that the target audience would use your company?

In the previous question, we were talking about the target audience when they were still prospects. They were asking the questions, "Why should I believe in you? Why should I move to the next step?" In this question, we are dealing with your customers, people who have already made a purchase with you. "What is the single-most compelling and competitive statement they will make?" Here are examples of how Nike Soccer and Dove Soap answer this question:

Nike Soccer: *I buy Nike shoes because they help me perform better, and they are worn by the best players in the world.*

Dove Soap: *Dove won't dry your skin like soap because it contains one-quarter moisturizing cream.*

Discriminator is an important one. I have read books and attended seminars on how to build your unique selling proposition (USP) or customer value proposition (CVP). I noticed that the exercises they took me through always generated "me-centric" USPs, which always referred to *our* company and how *we* were different from *our* competitors.

I love this brand and marketing positioning exercise because it focuses on how the *target audience* sees us. That is a significant paradigm shift if you really think about it. American companies (especially small businesses) tend to be very "self-focused." I'd like to encourage you to look at your business from your target audience's perspective. You will build a better brand for it.

This is why the question asks, "What is the single-most compelling statement that you would want the target audience to make about using your company?" Notice the question does not ask for the single, most competitive advantage *you* have in the marketplace.

Nike Soccer says, "We want people saying that they buy Nike shoes because they help them perform better and they are worn by the best players in the world." Dove Soap says, "We want people saying, 'Dove won't dry my skin like other soaps because it contains one-quarter moisturizing cream.'" These are very powerful brand discriminators. By the way, have you seen Dove's brand positioning exercise play itself out in advertising campaigns? The ad campaigns that led to millions of bars of soap being sold came out of a brand positioning exercise they did. The same will be true of you. Jot down all your thoughts on what a customer would say about your company.

Question Five: Competition—How do Prospects and Customers see your company in comparison to all the other choices available to them? Highlight the opportunities for specialization or targeting open to your company—and the threats where competitors are stronger!

We are carrying the customer-centric theme into this question. We are talking about customers who are evangelizing for, or promoting, your brand. They are talking to a friend, family member, or business associate about you. What would they say about your brand in comparison to others? Here are examples of how Swatch and Mercedes answer this question:

Swatch:	*Economy watches and fashion accessories that look great*
Mercedes:	*Luxurious and stately sedans*

Start to list your answers to Question Five. Which of the following would they say?

- "It's such a luxurious product."
- "It's a very economical product."
- "It saves me a ton of money."
- "They are the easiest to deal with."
- "This company really makes me feel good."
- "This company really helps me relax."

What would a customer be saying about you that also sends a message about how you stack up against the competition?

One of my favorite TV shows is *Top Gear* (the British version) on BBC America. If you like cars, you have to watch it yourself. In the show, these three so-funny-they'll-make-you-cry-laughing guys take super cars and put them through the paces on their race track. It is not uncommon for one of them to get out of a $200,000 super car and say "now that was lightning fast, but I'd rather be sitting on a pile of rocks than sitting in that awfully designed seat."

So if I worked at the auto manufacturer, I would be watching the show, clipboard in hand, saying: "Speed, check." "Comfort, uh-oh." "There's a competitor threat."

In one sense we are trying to identify opportunities where your company is perceived as the "lightning fast" option, the areas where your customer feels your company shines. However, we are also trying to identify the threats from competitors. What are those competitors doing better than us? This is where you don't want to have the blinders on.

It's one thing to say, "People are going to look at our business and say we are the best at everything." You know, I don't think that's possible. I'm a huge Apple product fan, but even they aren't perfect at everything. Be honest and identify the areas where you are going to be stronger than the competition. Then identify the areas where the competition could have an upper hand.

Question Six: Company Principles—What does your company stand for and believe in? What is its personality?

Remember when we kicked off this exercise, I suggested that every person has a set of core beliefs. They have a set of words that would describe who they are—friendly, outgoing, loving, caring, and trusting. You may describe your best friend or spouse that way. So how would you describe your business?

Here are examples of how Nike and Marlboro answer this question:

Nike:	*Inspire, Innovate, Connect, Focus, Care*
Marlboro:	*Masculinity, Freedom, Adventure*

Regardless of your views on the tobacco industry, they did build some pretty compelling brands. Marlboro said that their brand was about masculinity, freedom, and adventure. Now think about that for a minute. Think back to some of the Marlboro ads you probably saw before the tobacco industry took its hits. Remember those big Marlboro billboards and magazine spreads? It was a rugged cowboy with his horse, out on the open range. This is a perfect example of how advertising, marketing, and customer acquisition extract their identity from brand positioning.

In Table 13-3, you'll see the "Company Principles Pro Forma." There are more than 100 words there that should help jog your memory, if needed. But don't just go through this list and mark off your "Top 10." I want you to come up with your own words that really matter to you and that really define what your company is about. If you hit a creative block, look at the table for some inspiration. Don't be surprised if you end up with 15 or even 25 words or phrases that describe your company principles. Go for it. You can reduce and refine your list later.

Table 13-3 Company Principles Pro Forma

Accountability	Customer Focus	Information	Personal Growth
Achievement	Decisiveness	Hoarding	Power
Adaptability	Dialogue	Information	Pride
Adventure	Diversity	Sharing	Process Orientation
Attitude	Ease with	Initiative	Productivity
Authenticity	Uncertainty	Innovation	Product
Balance, Home/	Education	Integrity	Knowledge
Work	Efficiency	Interdependence	Profit
Being Liked	Empathy	Inventiveness	Quality
Being the Best	Empire Building	Job Security	Recognition
Blame	Enthusiasm	Knowledge	Reliability
Brand Focus	Entrepreneurship	Leadership	Respect
Bureaucracy	Environmental	Development	Reward
Caution	Awareness	Listening	Safety
Clarity	Ethics	Logic	Security
Coaching	Excellence	Long-Term	Shared Values
Commitment	External Competition	Prosperity	Shared Vision
Community Service	Extreme Loyalty	Loyalty	Shareholder
Compassion	Fairness	Making a	Value
Compromise	Family Atmosphere	Difference	Short-Term
Conflict Resolution	Financial Stability	Market Focus	Orientation
Conformity	Forgiveness	Mentoring	Skills Training
Consensus	Friendship	Open	Spirit
Continuity	Global Perspective	Communication	Stakeholder
Continuous	Goals Orientation	Openness	Satisfaction
Improvement	Health	Organizational	Teamwork
Continuous Learning	Honesty	Growth	Tenacity
Control	Human Rights	Passion	Tradition
Cooperation	Humility	Performance	Trust
Creativity	Humor/Fun	Perseverence	Vision
Customer	Image	Personal	Winning
Collaboration	Independence	Fulfillment	Wisdom

Question Seven: Company Essence—What single defining thought should be clearly recognizable in every aspect of your company, from the corner office to the factory floor and from marketing material to service provision?

Question Seven is the biggie for sure. It is your company essence. I want you to give me one clear thought and this should be recognizable in every aspect of your company. It should serve as a guide for telling you and your employees what is right and authentic for the brand—*and what is not.*

Here are examples of how Disney, Kellogg's, and Nike answer this question:

Disney:	*Magic you can believe*
Kellogg's:	*Sunshine vitality*
Nike:	*To bring inspiration and innovation to every athlete in the world*

Disney says, "We're about magic you can believe." Their entire business operates on the four words, *magic you can believe.* These words impact how they hire people, how they train them, how they market themselves, and what products they offer.

Nike says, "Our *ethos* is to bring inspiration and innovation to every athlete in the world." Now that's cool isn't it? When you think about Nike, you have to agree that's who they are. Their target audience is athletes. From super athletes, who make millions of dollars a year, to weekend warriors like me and young PeeWee football players, Nike wants to be part of our experience. Nike wants to inspire innovative products for their target audience.

Remember the "Just do it" Nike ads with Bo Jackson, and even some of the ads you see today? The ads are all about inspiring the athlete to get out there and do more, run faster, and achieve more. *Just do it.* That's the *inspiration* part. The *innovation* part consists of the new products that Nike brings into the market.

So what's your company's essence? What is the one statement you could create that would say this is *who we are* and *who we aren't*? Now, to get to this one statement, you'll probably write down 10. That's okay. This entire process is a brainstorming process. Write it all down.

Phew! We're almost done with Exercise Three. Just as in the previous exercise, I'd like you to leave your notes aside for a few days. Then come back to reduce and refine the notes to a single brand positioning statement.

Time to Transition

It's time to leave the confines of the owner's suite and bring your key team members in for the rest of the process. This would include any key advisors, management team, and mastermind team members. I'd recommend you start by presenting your paper napkin, your vision and mission statements, and your brand positioning statement to them. Use this meeting as an opportunity to cast your vision and get real-time feedback from the people who know you and your business better than anyone else. Be ready for open feedback and welcome it. This will put some final refinements on the foundational exercises.

Next, you are going to embark on a series of exercises with key members of your team. You can decide who needs to participate in each exercise, based on your company culture and the nature of the exercise. You can do these exercises in the course of a day or a day and a half (that's how I do it when I'm working with a client). However, you can also make this a four- to five-week project, with weekly meetings focused on one exercise each week. I'm a big fan of a weekend getaway or leadership retreats, where you can build synergy and get this done in one shot. However, this is just a personal preference.

chapter

14

Designing Your New Strategic Plan

Exercise Four: Optimizing the Business to Your Entrepreneurial DNA

Earlier, I took you through seven Business Optimization Strategies for your Primary Entrepreneurial DNA. Here is where you get to bring those strategies back and literally install them into the operating structure of your business and life.

In this exercise, you will present your Entrepreneurial DNA to your team. Tell them about the strengths, weaknesses, and frustrations of your Primary DNA. Describe any Secondary DNA you have. Teach them what you have learned about how the BOSI Quadrant works and how certain strengths and weaknesses are either enhanced or compensated for by other DNAs.

"But Joe, I'd be showing my team my dirty laundry," you say. Exactly!

Listen, I know plenty of CEOs who think they are demigods in their business. They assume that because they are owners, they have to appear omnipotent and omniscient. How is that working out for you so far?

The fact is, your team already *knows* most of your strengths and weaknesses. If you have a Primary Builder DNA, do you think they are going to be shocked and amazed when you talk about the Builder's ability to manipulate people and get them to do things they don't want to do? Take them out for a test drive and watch everyone grin and giggle as you describe your DNA. They already know!

Going through this exercise with them makes you more *transparent*. It proves to them that you are being *authentic* with them. They will respect you more for identifying your dirty laundry. Let me also assure you that the *right* ones will come alongside you and fill delivery gaps like they never had before. They will take ownership in your enterprise at a level you have never experienced. Remember my promise to you at the beginning of this journey? Here is what I said in the opening chapter:

> Your company will grow faster because you will be operating within your gifting, your staff and operations will be optimized around who you are, and your marketplace relationships will be maximized.

So do Exercise Four in full transparency and authenticity with your team, and I can assure you, I will have delivered on this promise.

The first thing you are going to do is a mini seminar on your Entrepreneurial DNA. Then talk about the seven strategies, one by one. Finally, let the team weigh in on which of the strategies need to be implemented and which strategies are already in place and performing well.

Here's an example. If you have a Primary Specialist DNA, I made seven strategy suggestions to you in Chapter 10:.

- Optimize your strategic plan
- Optimize your business development

- Optimize your advisory team
- Optimize your mastermind team
- Optimize your expert status
- Optimize your work–life balance plan
- Optimize your exit value potential

Let's consider Item five: Optimize your expert status, and dig into it.

You: "One of Joe's recommendations is that we build our expert status. Let's start by listing the things we do right now to build our expert status. Then we'll look at some of Joe's specific recommendations. Finally, we'll brainstorm some ideas of our own. The goal is for us to come up with a plan that makes sense. A plan that works for my Entrepreneurial DNA, our company, and our budget. But we want a plan that is in full alignment with our vision, mission, and brand position."

Team: "Right on! Let's do it" (or something to that effect).

Now let's consider item two, Optimize your business development, and dig into it.

You: "So based on the BOSI philosophy, standing out in a crowded marketplace is a constant struggle for companies like ours. We've got a couple of options here. We can come up with some fresh ideas of our own. That's Option One. Option Two is that we can bring in an expert who can help us craft an outside-the-box marketing plan that still fits my DNA. Option Three is that we just stay with what we have been doing because it is working just fine."

Team: "I/we vote for option _____."

It's fair to say you get the gist of what this exercise is all about so far.

Step One: Do the BOSI mini seminar.
Step Two: Go through the seven strategies.

The final step is to integrate the new plans that are optimized for your Entrepreneurial DNA into your business operation.

Keep in mind that this is still at the strategic planning and white-board level. You aren't running out to your factory floor making changes at this moment. You are simply finding places in your business that aren't optimized for your Entrepreneurial DNA and optimizing them.

For example, I recommend that all the BOSI DNAs have some sort of ongoing advisory and/or mastermind relationships. If we assume that you agree with the importance of this recommendation, it is at this point that you would look at your current modus operandi with advisory and/or mastermind relationships and come up with a new game plan.

Maybe you'll discover in Strategy Three for Specialist DNA that even though you currently mastermind with other business owners, that they are not the ideal group for you because you all have the same Primary DNA. Now is your opportunity to say, "Okay, in order to be optimized for my DNA, I need to go back to my group and suggest we split up into two groups—allowing a couple of new members to join each group—each with an opposing DNA."

Put differently, this is where you figure out the steps of what needs to be different in your new strategic plan. This is where you identify if you need to seek out a new business coach, digital marketing firm, business advisor, banking relationship, sales system, or marketing plan. Don't feel the pressure to identify the actual resource at this time. All you need to do right now is identify the need. We will get to the action plan in Exercise Seven.

So go through all seven strategies with your team and integrate them (strategically) into your business. Before you finish this session, make sure to do a final, mission-critical step. Take all the great, fresh, and new ideas that came out of this process and hold them up against your BOSI Entrepreneurial DNA, your vision and mission, and your market and brand positioning. Remember what I said earlier: your Entrepreneurial DNA, your vision and mission, and your market and brand positioning will become very powerful decision filters for you as (CEO). If you see something in the idea bin that conflicts with who you are, with your vision and mission, or with your market and brand positioning, toss it out.

This puts you miles ahead of competitors who will jump on every harebrained idea they read or hear about. With no filters, they will say yes to everything that sounds promising. You, on the other hand, will say yes to the things that will move you, your brand, and your company forward. However, you will say no to things that obviously conflict with those bedrocks.

Exercise Five: The A/B/C Scenarios

If you did Exercise Four correctly, the team will have come up with lots of great ideas to take to market. If you found yourself stalling out in Exercise Four, that is a great indication to bring in an expert who can help you design this integrated strategic plan. Either way, armed with all the great improvements, we have to evaluate how feasible those ideas are, given the time, talent, and resources your company possesses.

For example, if you've decided to really focus on building authority in your marketplace, you now have some decisions to make on how you are going to go about building that authority. You could do something as simple as set up a free blog where you demonstrate your content matter expertise. You could outsource to a digital marketing firm that deploys and manages the blog for you. Or you could go for the gold and hire a publicity expert to book you as an expert on Fox News and *The Today Show*. It all comes down to your appetite, resources, and risk tolerance.

The A/B/C Scenario exercise simply allows you to look at your options, put them on the table, and decide which rollout scenario is the right fit for you at this time.

- **Scenario A**—*The worst-case, minimum scenario:* What would your game plan look like if you just had to do the bare-bones stuff? As an example, in the area of building authority in your marketplace, Scenario A would look for the lowest cost/lowest risk options, such as setting up that free blog on blogger.com. When you get to the part of your strategy on building an advisory/mastermind team, the option of joining a free Meetup or LinkedIn group could fit well. Scenario A is nothing more than the lowest risk, lowest return version of your go-forward plan across all areas of your game plan.

- **Scenario B—*The realistic, average scenario:*** Here, you take things up a notch. Rather than set up a free blogger account, you may consider having an online marketing firm set up a Wordpress blog with a customized look and feel. A service like that can range from $1,500 to $3,500. That's why it falls in Scenario B. There's a greater cost than the Scenario A option. However, there could be a greater return given that your site will look and operate in a more robust fashion than the free blog in Scenario A. In Scenario B, rather than joining a free Meetup or LinkedIn group, you may consider joining a paid membership organization like a chamber of commerce or BNI International. Scenario B lays out the same overall game plan, but looks to allocate more resources in anticipation of a greater return.

- **Scenario C—*The best case, swing for the fences scenario:*** In this scenario, you spare no expense and go for the gold standard in every area of your deployment. This is a very important exercise to engage in because it is often an eye-opening experience. Remember, this is just an exercise. I am not asking you to pull out your checkbook and spend any money. All you are doing is war-gaming out the different plans of attack available to you. Here, you may look at what it would cost to have a digital marketing firm handling your entire online footprint on a full outsource basis. You may consider joining a high-end peer-advisory group like Vistage or Young Presidents' Organization (YPO). You may add in the investment to have a publicity expert get you recognized with local and regional press. If money was no object, what would your marketing plan, human resource (HR) systems, sales team, and company operations look like? That is Scenario C.

In each scenario, assign the investment you will need to make and the potential return on that investment. Here's an example of this process at work. In the case of a personal development company, we simply asked the following question, "If we needed to sell 10,000 books next year, what would we need to do as a business?" The answers across the various business areas became Scenario A.

Then we asked, "if we wanted to sell 50,000 books in the same period of time, what more would we need to do?" That became Scenario B.

Finally we asked, "if we wanted to sell 100,000 books in that same period of time, what would we need to do?" That became Scenario C.

Table 14-1 is a sample A/B/C Scenario output from that company. It will give you an idea of what the finished product of this exercise could look like.

When you complete your A/B/C Scenario exercise, your whiteboard, legal pad, or spreadsheet should give you a helicop-ter-level view of three very different paths to success. I want to emphasize why it is so important to look at all three scenarios, even though two of the three won't excite you much. The whole purpose of this process is for you to engage in strategic thought with your team, without any prejudgment of the solutions.

In a typical setting, you may not even have entertained the thought of some of the higher ticket items in Scenario C. However, going through the exercise of developing Scenario C stretches your creative and strategic muscle. A rubber band once stretched to a certain point never returns to its original size. If you are a Specialist or Innovator DNA, Scenario C should end up stretching you *far beyond* your comfort zone. If you are a Builder or Opportunist, Scenario A will be just as much of a stretch in the other direction.

Once you have the three possible rollout scenarios in place, you simply have to choose the one that best fits your company's current capacity. My guess is that unless you have completely

Table 14-1 A/B/C Scenario Output from a Personal Development Company

	A	B	C
Books sold*	10,000	50,000	100,000
Revenue potential†	$1 million	$5 million	$10 million
Staffing	Founders +3	Founders + 6	10 (outsource customer service)
Social media	In-house	Outsource set-up, in-house maintenance	Full outsource
Search engine optimization	None	Hire company for 1-time on page optimization	Full SEO service contract with top firm
Advertising‡	None	$4k per month	$8k per month
Events/shows	1/yr ($5,000)	4/yr ($25,000)	10/yr ($60,000)
CEO development (advisor/ mastermind)	Free stuff (Meetup and LinkedIn)	Join local networking organization	Engage a CEO coach/business advisor
Marketing plan development/ deployment	Founders	Founders with expert strategist to support	Full-time marketing executive with support team
Sales team	Founders	Founders + brokers/resellers	3 sales executives on staff
Deployment investment**	$10–15k	$75–100k	$250k

* In the case of this company, their main driver was going to be book sales. In your case it may be units of a product, visitors to your Web site, new clients, new recruits, or simply top-line revenue. Think about the key performance indicator your business will have for the next 3 years and build the A/B/C Scenarios around it.

† Revenue potential takes in the overall revenue the company could experience based on the sale of the primary driver. So in the case of this company, book sales led to seminar attendance, which led to coaching services and high-end consulting gigs. The revenue potential factors all those based on historical or projected conversion rates.

‡ Advertising number is based on what the company will have to spend to get to these revenues. Once these revenues were achieved, the numbers would increase proportional to revenue.

**Deployment investment is just a rough estimate of the amount of money the founders would have to put into the initiative before it was paying for itself.

disarmed or don't possess any Opportunist DNA, you will lean toward Scenario B or C. That decision may trigger the discussion about expanding your company's capacity to meet your new vision and strategic plan.

Expanding Your Capacity

The two main restraints on an entrepreneur's vision are human and financial capital. Given enough of both resources, an entrepreneur is capable of almost anything. The more human capital you have, the faster you can execute. The more financial capital you have, the more mistakes you can absorb. So as you stare head-on at the A/B/C Scenarios of where you want to take your company in the next chapter of its life, you may have to make the decision to expand your human or financial capital.

Human Capital

When it comes to expanding human capital, you have the choice of either staffing up or outsourcing. On a personal level and as a business advisor, I encourage entrepreneurs with Specialist, Innovator, and Opportunist DNA to focus more on outsourcing. I recommend this especially when it comes to marketing, accounting, and fulfillment.

"But the entrepreneur in me wants employees I can manage and control, Joe," you say.

I get that. But as Michael Gerber taught me in *The E-Myth* a long time ago, that's the easiest way to get stuck working *in* a business rather than working *on* it. I know too many entrepreneurs whose paper napkin called for them to be a world-traveling, family vacationing, absentee business owner. Yet they find themselves running staff meetings, putting out fires, and managing lines of credit to cover their payroll account.

Here's another reason I would advise you to consider outsourcing for any expanded human capacity needs. Look at the rate at which our world is changing. Unless you have your employees in school 40 percent of the time keeping up with all the changes taking place technologically, socially, politically, and economically, they will fall behind. In the past few years, I have seen such highly skilled, high-output outsource companies emerge in the U.S. market that I can't help but tell my clients to consider using them.

For example, I was recently on the phone with a guy who had worked with some of the largest banks in the world. Then he spent almost a decade with a large venture capital fund. Finally, he became an angel investor himself. Along the way, he discovered the gaping hole within most start-ups for sound chief financial officer (CFO) level expertise. Most start-ups simply can not afford a full-time, high-pedigree CFO. So he set up a company that allows a start-up to access his level of expertise for the cost of a bookkeeper each month. For a few hundred extra dollars, his company manages the start-up's entire financial system *remotely*— from accounts payables and accounts receivables to collections, bookkeeping, and tax planning. It's all done for the start-up, but most importantly, the start-up has a part-time CFO who has the experience, pedigree, and Rolodex to help it attract the investors it is going to need in the future. How can a $40,000 per year bookkeeper compete with that level of service?

The same applies to online marketing. I have walked the halls of many Builder/Specialist companies as they proudly display their marketing departments. They have Web designers, copywriters, and even someone doing search engine optimization (SEO) and blogging. You know what I'm thinking in my head as I walk the halls? "I know digital marketing entrepreneurs who will 'eat this team's lunch' any day of the week and twice on Saturday."

Add it up with me for a minute. Staff, equipment, bandwidth, insurance, office space (the list goes on) versus the $2,500 to $7,500 per month that it would cost you to hire an outsource firm to do it all for you.

There are some areas of your business where you may have to expand internal capacity. However, first look for ways to expand your capacity externally. It involves less risk, better quality results, and faster speed to market.

Financial Capacity

I like reading poll results on content aggregators like Yahoo Finance, Fox Small Business, and *Entrepreneur* magazine. They always post the cutest poll questions like, "What's the no. 1 need your business has right now?"

Eager entrepreneurs answer in overwhelming majority that *cash* is their no. 1 need. "If I only had the working capital to _____ (fill in the blank), I'd build my company to the stars," they say.

Really? The last three small businesses I spent a day with (who had the same "I need money" song playing) would have gone out of business with more capital. In other words, their pricing structure was flawed to a point that new business would have aggravated an already problematic cash flow challenge. If you are losing money when you sell your service (but don't even know it), more growth capital is *not* the solution. The only reason I share this is to caution you, the entrepreneur, to make sure the demand for capital is coming from more than just the Opportunist DNA in you.

Make sure you have consulted with external advisors who can confirm that your business model, pricing structure, and financial systems are ready and able to handle an infusion of cash while providing the funding source with the return on investment (ROI) they will expect. With that said, let's talk about some ways to expand financial capacity based on your Entrepreneurial DNA.

If you have a Primary Builder DNA, consider equity or debt financing. If your Builder DNA is very strong, then consider a blend of equity and debt financing. Debt will be the cheapest money you will be able to access, given the rate at which you will create shareholder value.

If you have a Primary Specialist DNA, debt financing is the only realistic option for you. Unless you end up tapping the Builder or Opportunist in you, chances are you will not build a very scalable enterprise. As a result, traditional investors will not see the potential for the type of return they are used to getting. As an added bonus to the debt financing option, your methodical and structured work environment will give your lender plenty of peace of mind. Put another way, the Specialist in you will diligently pay the note back.

If you have a Primary Innovator DNA, equity financing is the way to go. However, a smart investor isn't going to write you a check directly. The investor will wait until you have a capable management team in place before doing so. Focus on building your team *before* asking for capital.

Finally, if you are a Primary Opportunist DNA, financing is going to be a challenge . . . period. The higher your Opportunist DNA score, the lower your funding chances. Your projections will be too optimistic, your assumptions will probably be half-baked, and the odds of you sticking around long enough to build the company to success will be so low that you are setting yourself and your lender/investor up for disappointment. Keep that in mind as you go asking for financing. Put people and systems in place *ahead of time* that will give your financiers the peace of mind and confidence they will need to pull out their checkbooks.

"So if I'm an Opportunist, are you saying I'm out of luck on funding, Joe?" you ask.

No, I have good news. The good news is that there is a highly targeted group you can raise tons of money with. It is other Opportunists. The higher their Opportunist score, the more likely you will get them excited about your mission. Focus on them for your funding and you will do just fine. (If you are a seasoned Opportunist, you figured this strategy out a long time ago and you are probably smiling as you read this part.)

Regardless of your DNA or funding source, the no. 1 question your funding source is going to have is this:

"What is the money going to be used for and when can I get it back?"

The good news is that the strategic plan you are building and the next two exercises you are about to do will give you the answer to that question. As a reminder to close out Exercise Five, you need to pick the scenario (A, B, or C) that you are going to deploy into the marketplace.

Exercise Six: The Three-Year Pro Forma

Now that you have chosen Scenario A, B, or C, it is time to build a more formalized version of your projections than the quick-and-dirty version you did in the previous exercise. This is a great exercise to do with your finance manager or outsourced accountant. Simply take the scenario that won in the previous exercise and flesh out a three-year projected profit and loss statement. Take the time to carefully consider all the costs that will be involved in accomplishing the sales and revenues you are projecting. Once built, this three-year pro forma will accomplish several objectives.

1. The pro forma becomes the navigation system for your finance team as it plans cash flow and manages revenues and expenses.
2. It becomes a means for you to be held accountable to your board, shareholders, investors, and/or lenders for the execution of the plan you have set forth.
3. Most importantly, it helps you predict the capital you may need to infuse to get the desired result, as well as the company's ability to generate a return on that investment for you or your funding source.

The three-year pro forma also acts as a gut-check for you, the entrepreneur, as you give the final go or no-go decision for the rollout of the strategic plan. Much like a pilot reviews a flight plan and compares it to other variables including weather, passenger load, and air traffic, you need to take a good hard look at the three-year pro forma and decide how doable it is. Only you will have the perspective to decide if the plan is a go.

Your accountant will think it is risky. Your staff will think it is too much new work. Your peers may cautiously encourage you. Take all their input in as part of your decision. However, use your

BOSI profile, your vision and mission, and your market and brand positioning filters to make the ultimate decision.

I hope you will be at the peak of your excitement as you look at this three-year pro forma. All the work you have done to this point is culminating itself into an intentional growth strategy that has integrated your Entrepreneurial DNA into it.

Exercise Seven: The 90-Day Action Plan

The journey of a thousand miles begins with a single step, right? So the final exercise we are doing together simply takes the three-year strategic plan and asks this simple question:

> "What do we have to do in the next 90 days to be right on track to achieve our three-year plan?"

Since this is the first 90 days of the deployment, there will be many one-time tasks that need to take place. Many of these tasks will involve planning and preparation.

Think in terms of remodeling a home. Long before you go to purchase new fixtures and begin to install them, you have to build your team and set a project plan. This exercise is simply that project planning process. Look at all the moving parts you talked about in Exercises Four, Five, and Six. Across each of the business units involved, what do each of them need to accomplish in the first 90 days?

Depending on how far off course you were from your Entrepreneurial DNA, you may need 90 to 180 days just to get your current operation restructured around who you are. If so, focus on that first. If you need help, call in an expert. The action steps you create become the tasks on your first 90-day action plan. Don't feel like you have to engage in the new elements of your go-to-market strategy until the proper internal foundation has been laid.

So as part of building your 90-day action plan, you have to ask:

1. **What needs to be done?** From optimizing operations and interviewing potential outsource vendors to raising capital

and revamping your Web site. List every single task that needs to take place.

2. **Who needs to do it?** Assign a person to oversee each task on the list. If needed, add a layer of accountability and/or oversight for that person.

3. **How long should it take, what are the interdependencies, and how much of our resources do we need to allocate to it?** These are typical project planning questions that need to be asked so that the first 90-day plan can have a very firm set of deliverables and expectations.

Once you have your first 90-day plan in place, you will be ready to *deploy* that plan in the marketplace. If you have optimized your company for your Entrepreneurial DNA, then there will be experts, advisors, and peer group members supporting you and holding you accountable for the execution of the plan. Don't go it alone. Make sure a strong team— of internal and external people—is going to be part of the journey with you.

If you feel the urge, pull the entire team together for a half-day summit or a one- hour Webinar and walk them through the entire strategic plan. Start with your foundational items like vision and mission, and market and brand positioning. Talk about the systems in your business that will be optimized to your Entrepreneurial DNA. Tell them about your commitment to maintain balance between business and personal life. Talk through the strengths of your Entrepreneurial DNA and how you plan to leverage them. Talk also about the weaknesses of your Entrepreneurial DNA and how specific team members (current or future) will offset those weaknesses. Lay out the vision for the next three years. Show your team the three-year pro forma. Finally, talk them through the first 90-day action plan.

You'll find yourself and your team getting energized to get out there and execute a competition-crushing game plan. For the first time ever, this game plan will be built around you. It will have all the elements of sound strategy, quality people, healthy accountability, and balance.

chapter

15

The Real Journey Is About to Begin

One of the biggest questions I get when I am talking to entrepreneurs is, "Is any one BOSI Profile combination better than the others?" As much as I've tried to find the "perfect" combination to date, I have not. There are millionaire and billionaire entrepreneurs in each of the four areas of our BOSI Quadrant. There are also bankrupt entrepreneurs in each area. I can tell you that 100 percent of any one DNA is less to be desired than being a combination. I find entrepreneurs with multiple DNAs to be a bit more balanced and more open to change and improvement than a purebred.

The thing I love the most about entrepreneurship is that we come in all shapes and sizes. Some of us want to build the next Google. Others want nothing to do with that commitment and would much rather own home-based, lifestyle-friendly, online-marketing businesses. Then, in between, there are the rest of us.

If I could engineer the perfect entrepreneur, he or she would have the best traits of all four BOSI DNAs. This entrepreneur would have the Builder's skill of system design and problem solving, and the Opportunist's big-vision, *anything is possible* optimism. I'd ensure that this engineered entrepreneur would have the methodical expertise and focus of the Specialist, and the ground-breaking ingenuity of the Innovator.

But what would we have accomplished by concocting such a lab freak? Exactly that—a freak. I am reminded of the character of Data in *Star Trek: The Next Generation*. His designer thought Data was the perfect machine. He built Data with perfect intelligence and super-human strength. Data was thought to have all the desirable characteristics one could ever want (much like many of the superheroes we grew up with). But the superheroes' creators built flaws into their characters. Every one of the superheroes or superheroines we know of had a weakness somewhere.

So when someone asks me the question, "What is the best BOSI Profile?" my answer is simple:

"The best BOSI Profile is the one you already have as long as you have optimized your business according to the strengths and weaknesses of your particular DNA."

On a personal level, my frustrations, weaknesses, and shortfalls in business simply remind me that I am just another "dog playing in the dog park" of entrepreneurship. Sure, some other dogs are faster, fiercer, and even smarter than I am. But I have a valuable contribution I can make given my unique gifts. Rather than pick a fight with the other dogs in the dog park, I have found that it is better to have fun with them and build community together.

"You Say Good-bye and I Say Hello"

We are at the end of our time together, but your real journey is just beginning. I hope you have found this book to be educational, informative, and somewhat inspirational. Remember, the thesis statement given at the end of Chapter 3:

"Best results in business come after you have mastered your Entrepreneurial DNA and optimized your business plan for your unique gifts, strengths, and weaknesses."

As you have read through the book, I hope that you have identified red light areas in your business where you were implementing *someone else's* game plan and paying the price for it. I hope that you have identified things you *were* doing in your business that you are going to do a bit differently now. I'm sure that you also found areas where you had intuitively optimized areas of business for your Entrepreneurial DNA.

I hope your brain is gushing with ideas you want to implement—beginning with drafting up a whole new game plan for the next chapter in your entrepreneurial journey. Whether you are about to start up a company, take an existing company to the next level of success, or put your exit plan into action, strategy is *everything*.

I commend that process to you as a follow-up to the seeds that have been planted along your reading journey. If you need help or guidance in building your go-forward strategic plan, there is a deep well of resources and relationships waiting at the BOSI Web site designed to help you get the best results possible.

They say the journey of a thousand miles begins with a single step. It is time to take the first step. If you happened to speed through this book the first time without stopping to do the exercises, please don't let this book get parked on a book shelf somewhere. If you need a pep talk or a helping hand, give us a shout. Your business and life deserve the best possible results.

I believe they deserve *breakthrough* results. I hope I get to meet you someday and shake your hand. (Hugs are okay too.) May God bless you.

$\left[\ \text{a p p e n d i x}\ \ \text{a}\ \right]$

The SPACE
Marketing Funnel

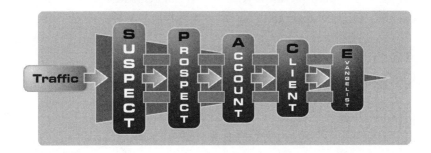

Get rid of all the complicated marketing systems these so-called marketing gurus are teaching out there today. Just look at the simple graphic above and build your marketing funnel around it. I was first introduced to a variation of this concept by a marketing consultant named Jon Eklof from the Minneapolis, MN, area.

Suspects

Suspects are your target audience (see questions 1 and 2 in the market/brand positioning exercise). Answering those questions correctly will give you a very clear picture of who your suspects are. Suspects are anonymous. They are simply members of your target audience. They fit the description of the type of consumer who would *potentially buy* your product or service.

Prospects

The next group in the marketing funnel is your *prospects*. A prospect is someone who came out of the suspect pool and raised his or her hand to say, "I am ready to talk to you." Prospects fill out a form on your Web site, or call your toll-free number, or send you an e-mail. But a series of events around their needs, timing, and your marketing efforts coincided in such a way that they said, "I am ready for more information." Finding suspects and converting them to prospects is all about having a finely tuned marketing and lead generation machine.

Question: What systems do you have in place to find suspects and convert them into prospects? What resources have you placed out there that allow suspects to get educated and informed enough to be willing to raise their hands and become prospects?

Accounts

Once you have a prospect, the next step is to make that prospect a first-time buyer—we call them accounts. These accounts are prospects who have reached into their pockets and pulled out a dollar to hand you in exchange for your product or service. This step is less about marketing and much more about selling. The quality of your sales process and your salespeople will determine how many prospects turn into accounts—first-time buyers.

Clients

After we have an account, the next step is to turn that first-time buyer into a repeat buyer. We call repeat buyers *clients*. I think we can agree that this process of converting first-time buyers into clients is critical because most of our profits come from our clients. When you look at the amount of money it takes to find suspects, convert them into prospects, go through the sales and follow-up process to make them into accounts—then pay selling costs and commissions and cover overhead—we're fortunate if we break even on that initial sale. The profits come when that same account buys again, and again, and again.

So take a look at your business development engine and ask what systems are in place to move someone from first time buyer to repeat buyer without requiring you to "remember to do it."

Evangelists

The final step is to convert clients into evangelists. I don't have to explain this one much, do I? We all know who evangelists are. They are our fanatical fans who can't stop talking about us. Every business has evangelists. It's just that you and I just wish we had *more* of them. Well, there is something that you can do about it. Most businesses sit back and wait for evangelists to appear. Great businesses like Apple and Google invest in and *build* evangelists. It is part of their strategic plan. There are steps they engage in to make sure a certain percentage of clients turn into evangelists.

Traffic

Design your business development engine around the SPACE graphic above. Once you, the owner, have the confidence that the proper systems are in place, tuned up, and ready to hit the track, then and only then should you spend money to advertise and drive *traffic* to the engine.

It all comes down to systems—and that is the take-away no.1 I wanted to have for you. Ask yourself this question: What systems do I have in place to find suspects, convert them into prospects, sell them into accounts, upgrade them into clients, and build them into evangelists? Is your business development engine a set of systems, or are *you* the business development engine? If you want to learn more about SPACE, there are tons of additional resources waiting for you at the BOSI Web site.

The Credibility Analyzer
for Opportunist DNA

Name of the individual I am assessing:_____.

My relationship to this individual: _____.

Please select only *one* answer per question.

1. **On the 1–10 scale below, what is your perception of this individual's business skill?**

    *   1–3 (very low skill—this individual should not be doing business on his or her own)
    *   4–6 (average skill—this individual could do well with some good support)
    *   7–9 (above-average skill—this individual is likely to do quite well in business)
    *   10 (extremely high skill—this person is a "rock star" when it comes to business)

2. **How much do you trust this individual's ability to find a good business opportunity that is safe and reputable?**

   - I don't think this individual has the nose to recognize a good opportunity
   - I think this individual has a good nose for the right opportunities
   - I don't know

3. **If this individual was investing in a business, how likely would you be to invest with them?**

   - Very likely
   - Somewhat likely
   - Not likely

4. **How credible is this individual with you when it comes to business matters?**

   - I trust this individual's ideas and insight a great deal. I consider them an expert.
   - I find this individual's ideas and insights interesting but don't agree with them.
   - I don't consider this individual to be credible in business.

5. **Leadership: How do respect this individual as a leader?**

   - Yes, this individual is a strong leader who I would follow.
   - No, this individual is not a leader I would follow.

6. **Improvement: The no. 1 thing I would want this individual to do to improve is:**

   - To focus on one business at a time.
   - To spend less time dreaming and more time doing.

- To get a full-time job.
- To be more patient with his or her business venture.
- To get some help, training, support.
- To find a business partner.
- Other: (Please describe)_____

_____

[a p p e n d i x c]

The Relationship Analyzer for Builder DNA

Name of the individual I am assessing: _____

My relationship to this individual: _____

Please select only *one* answer per question.

1. **General Temperament: How would you describe the general temperament (mood) of this individual?**

   - Always calm and composed
   - Generally calm with occasional outbursts of anger
   - Very unpredictable. I'm always on eggshells around this person
   - Always mean and angry

2. **Communication: What is it like when you are communicating with this individual?**

- This individual always engages in the conversation with me. I feel like I am being heard and understood.
- This individual usually engages in the conversation with me. However, sometimes I don't feel that I have really been heard or understood.
- It's very hard to connect. Most of the time, I feel like this individual is not even listening to what I am saying and seems to be thinking about something else more important.

3. **Asking for help: How comfortable are you asking this individual for help when you need it?**

- I feel very comfortable approaching this individual for help. This individual is always willing to help me.
- I feel fairly comfortable, but every once in a while I get the feeling that my remarks are bothering this individual.
- I feel intimidated asking for help. I get the feeling that this individual is too busy for me.

4. **Quality time: Do you get the amount of quality time you want with this individual?**

- I get plenty of one-on-one quality time with this individual.
- I don't get much one-on-one quality time with this individual.
- I am starved for one-on-one quality time with this individual.

5. **Priorities: What's more important to this individual, people or business?**

   - It appears as though the business is a much higher priority to this individual than people are.
   - Business and people are equal.
   - This person values people far more than the business.

6. **Leadership Style: How do you perceive this individual's leadership style?**

   - Authoritarian—the individual controls everyone and everything. It's definitely a dictatorship around here.
   - Authoritative—This individual is a strong leader but is very open to input.
   - Servant Leadership—This individual does not lead—the opposite of authoritarian.

7. **Powerful vs. Forceful: How does this person get people to do things?**

   - This person can get me to do things I wouldn't normally do and I appreciate him or her for it.
   - This person has made me a better person.
   - This person can get me to do things I wouldn't normally do, but I resent the manner in which she or he does it.
   - This person has overused his or her influence by manipulating me too many times. I am quite fed up.

8. **Improvement: The no. 1 thing I would want this individual to change/improve is:**

   - To slow down and spend more quality time with me and others.

- Not be so obsessed with business but have more work-life balance.
- Make healthier choices. I am concerned about this individual's health.
- Be more patient with me and others when we make mistakes.
- Not try to control everything and everyone so much.
- Not fly off the handle so easily. To be kinder in how she or he interacts with me.
- Other: (Please describe.)

index